Ancient
Greece

000 FACTS

First published in 2008 by Miles Kelly Publishing Ltd
Bardfield Centre, Great Bardfield, Essex, CM7 4SL

This material is also available in hardback

2 4 6 8 10 9 7 5 3 1

Editorial Director Belinda Gallagher
Art Director Jo Brewer
Editor Rosalind McGuire
Editorial Assistant Carly Blake
Page Layout Rick Caylor, Ian Paulyn
Picture Researcher Laura Faulder
Production Manager Elizabeth Brunwin
Indexer Hilary Bird
Reprographics Anthony Cambray, Ian Paulyn

British Library Cataloguing-in-Publication Data
A catalogue record for this book is available from the British Library

ISBN 978-1-84236-957-9

Printed in China

www.mileskelly.net
info@mileskelly.net

www.factsforprojects.com

Ancient Greece

1000 FACTS

Rupert Matthews

Miles Kelly

PUBLISHING

Contents

Contents

SCIENCE AND THE ARTS

GODS AND FESTIVALS

Prehistoric Greece

- **Modern Greece** covers only part of the area that was inhabited by the Greeks in ancient times. From around 700 BC the ancient Greeks spread over much of what is now southern Italy, Turkey and lands around the Black Sea.

- **In prehistoric times** (until around 2000 BC), the higher mountains were covered with forests of oak, pine and ash.

- **Humans have lived** in Greece for about half a million years. People belonging to the same species as modern humans arrived in Greece about 75,000 years ago.

- **About 5000 years ago**, these peoples learned how to plant grain crops such as wheat and barley, and how to grow fruits such as plums and grapes. They began to live as farmers.

- **About the year 2000 BC**, a new group of people began to move into Greece from the north and northeast. These people were the Hellenes, the ancestors of the Greeks.

- **The Hellenes** were pastoralists, meaning that they herded cattle, horses and sheep. As they settled in Greece they began to live in villages and farm food crops.

- **Herds of goats and sheep** brought to Greece by the Hellenes grazed on the leaves and shoots of young trees and so stopped them growing. Gradually the forests were destroyed.

- **By around 1800 BC**, the Hellenes had settled across most of mainland Greece and its nearby islands. They were now more numerous than the original inhabitants of these lands.

- **During this period**, tools and weapons were made from stone and bronze.

THRACE
Byzantium
MACEDONIA
PHRYGIA
Aegean Sea
Larissa
THESSALY
EPIRUS
Corcyra
Pergamon
Ionian Sea
LYDIA
Sardis
AETOLIA
BOEOTIA
Delphi
Thebes
ATTICA
Athens
Ephesus
Corinth
Mycenae
Olympia
Argos
Delos
PELOPONNESE
Sparta
Rhodos
Mediterranean Sea
CRETE

▲ *Ancient Greek cities were widely spread across what is now Turkey, and some colonies were to be found as far west as Spain.*

- **The prehistoric Greeks** lived in small towns, each of which ruled the surrounding areas of farmland and mountains. Some of these towns grew large enough to be called cities.

The Mycenaean Period

- **By about 1750** BC, the most important city in Greece was Mycenae. Modern historians refer to this period of Greek history as the Mycenaean Period. This lasted until around 1150 BC.

- **Other important cities** at this time included Iolkos, Tiryns, Pylos, Dyme, Delphi, Athens, Thebes and Orchomenos. Each city was independent of the others, and there may have been over 100.

- **Cities were surrounded** by strong walls made from large, irregular-shaped blocks of stone. These provided defence against attack. Some cities had spectacular gateways.

▲ *A golden mask found in a royal tomb at Mycenae dating to about 1400 BC. Mycenae was one of the largest and most powerful cities in Greece at that time.*

- **Most people lived** on the land as farmers or herdsmen, and many fishermen lived along the coast. Few people earned a living by making things to sell.

- **There was no money** in Mycenaean Greece. Instead, people swapped what they had for things they wanted. For example, a farmer might have swapped a quantity of food for a vase.

- **During this time**, the Greeks appear to have lived only along the coasts of the southern and eastern parts of what is now Greece, and also on some of the nearby islands.

- **Around 1450 BC**, the Greeks developed a system of writing. The early script they used is known as Linear A, but it is unlike later Greek script, and has not yet been fully deciphered.

- **People used** pointed pieces of wood to carve letter symbols into small tablets of wet clay. The clay could then be smoothed over and used again if necessary.

- **From about 1080 to 750 BC**, Greece entered a period now referred to as the Dark Age. During this time the history of the Mycenaean Period was lost. Later legends preserve stories about these times, some of which were probably based on fact.

...FASCINATING FACT...
If a clay tablet needed to be kept permanently it was fired like a pot. Some tablets were preserved accidentally after they became fired in a burning building.

The bull of Minos

- **During the Mycenaean Period** on mainland Greece, a different civilization flourished on the island of Crete. This civilization is known as Minoan, from the name of a legendary king of Crete – Minos.

- **The most important palace** on Minoan Crete was Knossos in the north. Other palaces included Kydonia in the west, Phaistos in the south and Kato Zakro in the east.

- **Temples and other important buildings** of Minoan Crete were decorated with pictures and sculptures of bull horns. It is thought that these people may have worshipped a bull god.

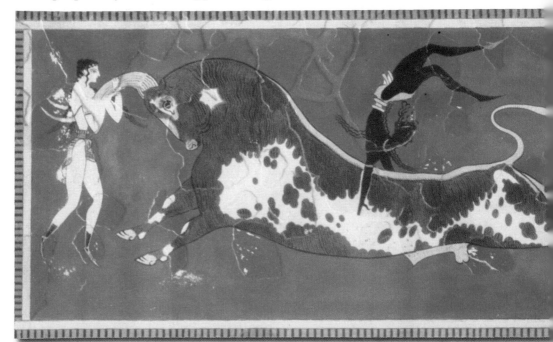

- **One fresco shows** young men jumping over the back of a charging bull. This may have been a dangerous sport, or some form of worship of the bull god.

- **Merchants from Crete** sailed to Syria, Egypt and mainland Greece to trade for goods such as bronze tools, olive oil and papyrus (a form of paper). The Minoans grew rich as a result.

- **Minoan merchants** also traded with other travellers who had come from further away. They imported amber from the Baltic Sea and ivory from Africa.

- **The Minoans** left writings in strange scripts, known as Linear A and Phaistos Disc.

- **Both of these scripts** remain undeciphered today, so we do not know what the writings mean.

- **Around 1625** BC, Crete was hit by a tidal wave caused by a massive volcanic eruption on the island of Thera. Many cities and homes were destroyed. It is possible that this eruption was the reason why the Minoan civilization went into decline.

- **About the year 1450** BC, Crete was taken over by Greek kings from the mainland. They introduced Mycenaean weapons and art styles, but also retained much of the Minoan culture.

◀ *A fresco (wall painting) found at Knossos, Crete. It shows a group of young men leaping acrobatically over a charging bull, an animal thought to be sacred to the Minoans.*

13

The Trojan War

- **Troy was a mighty city** in the country of Illios in what is now northwestern Turkey. It controlled trade routes to the Black Sea, becoming one of the richest cities in the ancient world.

- **Ancient records show** that the Trojans fought several wars against raiders from Mycenaean Greece. Archaeologists have found that the city was invaded and destroyed around 1180 BC.

- **According to later Greek legends**, Troy was destroyed after a war that lasted ten years. All the kings of Mycenaean Greece then joined forces to attack Troy, sailing across the Aegean Sea in a fleet of 1000 ships.

- **It was believed** that the Trojan War began when Paris, son of King Priam of Troy, fell in love with Queen Helen of Sparta. He abducted her and took her away to Troy. Helen's husband, King Menelaus, asked his brother, King Agamemnon of Mycenae, for help.

- **Agamemnon summoned** the Greek kings to attack Troy. Among those who came were Odysseus of Ithaca and the warrior-hero Achilles.

- **When Achilles fought**, the Greeks were much stronger than the Trojans, but after an argument with Agamemnon, Achilles stayed in his tent and refused to fight. The Trojans began to win victories.

- **When Achilles' friend Patroclus** was killed by the Trojan Hector, Achilles left his tent. He killed Hector in single combat then rejoined the fighting. The Trojans fell back behind their city walls.

- **Odysseus suggested** that the Greeks pretend to give up and go home, leaving behind a large wooden horse as a gift to the gods. In fact, the horse contained Greek warriors and the Greek army was only a short distance away.

- **The Trojans** pulled the horse into Troy.
  That night the hidden warriors leapt
  out and opened the city gates. Troy
  was captured by the Greeks.

- **After the war**, Helen returned to
  Sparta. Troy was later resettled,
  but was never again
  as rich and powerful
  as it had been.

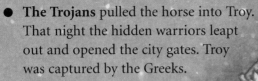

◄ *Greek soldiers
emerge from the
wooden horse inside
which they have
been hiding. Legend
says that the city of
Troy was captured
after a long war in
about 1180 BC.*

The fall of the palaces

▲ *The entrance to a huge tomb just outside Mycenae, now known as the Treasury of Atreus.*

- **Around the year 1200 BC**, the eastern Mediterranean world entered a troubled time, and the cities of Mycenaean Greece began to decline.

- **Later Greek legends** blamed feuds within the ruling families of Mycenae and other cities for the economic decline.

- **Around 1190** BC, Egypt was attacked by a mass of invaders who arrived by sea from the north. At first, the Egyptians referred to the invaders as 'Sea Peoples', but later learned that the people referred to themselves as Sherdan, Peleset and Denyen.

- **Pharaoh Rameses III** defeated the first invasion by the Sea Peoples, but later invasions caused massive damage to Egypt.

- **Around the same time** the Hittite Empire collapsed. The Hittites ruled most of what is now Turkey. The collapse was so sudden that no records of the events survived.

- **In about 1120** BC, the city of Mycenae was destroyed by fire. After the fire, the city was abandoned completely, so it is possible that the destruction was caused by a war.

- **Many other cities** of Mycenaean Greece were also abandoned around that time. Some were left in ruins, while others, such as Athens, survived as smaller towns.

- **One document from Pylos** records that extra soldiers were sent out on patrol just before the city was destroyed. Few other written records from other cities survived the destruction.

- **Modern historians** think that a period of economic decline and poor harvest was followed by an invasion by a Greek-speaking people called the Dorians.

- **The kings** of Mycenaean Greece had failed in their most important duty – to protect their lands and people. The whole culture collapsed and a 'Dark Age' began in Greece.

The Dark Age

- **By about 1080** BC, the Mycenaean civilization had completely collapsed. There are no written records from this time and very few archaeological remains have been found. This period is known as the Greek Dark Age.

- **During this time**, small groups of people roamed Greece and nearby lands trying to find suitable areas for settlements. Some of these migrations formed the basis of later legends.

- **One group of Dorians** settled in the valley of the Eurotas River and became rulers of the city state of Sparta. Spartan records indicate that this happened in 1102 BC.

▶ *A large ornamental jar dating to the Dark Age of Greece. Decoration in horizontal lines was very popular during this period.*

- **Another group** of Dorians conquered Crete in about 1020 BC. They appointed themselves kings and nobles, and ruled over the native inhabitants.

- **A large number of Greeks** from around Athens fled from the Dorians. They settled on the western coast of what is now Turkey and called themselves Ionians after their first king, Ion.

- **Poetry was highly admired** as an art form during the Dark Age. Two long poems in the epic tradition dating from the Dark Age were later written down. They are called *Illiad* and *Odyssey*.

- *Illiad* and *Odyssey* are concerned with the Trojan War and its aftermath, and they were passed down through oral tradition for generations. They are traditionally considered to have been given their final form by a poet called Homer.

- **Homer** is believed to have lived in Ionia, possibly around 800 BC. Very little is known about his life, but it is traditionally thought that he became a poet as a way to earn a living because he was blind and unable to work at other trades. Some scholars deny that Homer ever existed.

- **During the Dark Age**, a new style of pottery developed in Greece. It featured simple patterns of squares, circles and straight lines and this style became known as Geometric. It was a departure from the earlier Mycenean style of pottery, which was more decorative.

- **Iron was introduced** to Greece during the Dark Age. At first, the metal was very expensive, so it was used only by kings and nobles.

A new dawn

- **After about 750 BC**, the Dark Age ended in Greece. Life became more settled and people became more prosperous as the economy of the eastern Mediterranean began to flourish once again.

- **At this time**, the most important cities in Greece included Sparta, Athens, Thebes, Megara, Paros and Askra. Many of the important cities of the Mycenaean period had fallen into ruin.

- **By 700 BC**, most cities were dominated by a small number of rich families. The Greeks called these families aristoi, meaning 'the best', from which we get our modern word – aristocrat.

- **The aristocrats** owned most of the best farm land. They did not farm the land themselves, but hired farmers and bought slaves to do the work for them.

- **Fine pottery** began to be made in Corinth and other cities. The remains of these vases and bowls have been found by archaeologists and illustrate the increasing wealth and sophistication of Greece.

▶ *Fast-moving chariots carrying armed men could race around the battlefield to exploit weaknesses in an enemy army or to cover retreats. For centuries men riding in chariots were the key weapon in Greek warfare.*

About the year 700 BC, a farmer from Boeotia (a region of ancient Greece north of Corinth) named Hesiod began writing poetry. His work poked fun at the aristocrats and celebrated hardworking farmers.

- **Horses were expensive** in ancient Greece because grazing land was scarce. Aristocrats showed off their wealth by owning and riding horses. They even gave their children names such as Philip, which means 'horse-lover'.

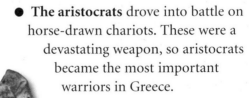

- **The aristocrats** drove into battle on horse-drawn chariots. These were a devastating weapon, so aristocrats became the most important warriors in Greece.

- **Aristocrats did not need** to work for a living. They were free to act as judges in the law courts, generals during wartime and government officials during peacetime.

- **Some aristocrats worked hard** without pay for the good of the people of their cities.

Tyrants and lawgivers

- **By about 650 BC**, many Greek cities were threatened with political crisis as a result of developments in battle techniques.

- **A new style** of fighting emerged. Lower class men began to fight in tight formations wearing hoplite armour of a shield, helmet, spear and sword. Using this method they were able to defeat the chariots of the aristocrats.

- **As a result** of their new success in battle, the lower classes wanted political power. The aristocrats thought the positions for lower class men should be restricted to part-time officials, and they refused to hand over power. Political disputes began, which sometimes turned into civil war.

- **Some cities** entered what the Greeks called *stasis*. This meant that the citizens were so busy arguing over who should rule the city that working and trading ground to a halt.

- **About the year 750 BC**, a prince of Sparta named Lycurgos was given the power to reform the constitution of the city to solve the disputes between the aristocrats and the citizens.

- **While other cities** entered *stasis*, Sparta remained orderly and prosperous. The constitution invented by Lycurgos, and developed by later kings, ensured stability.

- **Other cities decided** to copy Sparta and appoint one respected man to reform their constitutions. These men became known as the lawgivers.

- **In 594 BC**, Athens appointed a poet named Solon as their lawgiver. Solon was so effective that he later travelled to other cities to give advice on lawmaking.

- **In other cities**, the disputes led to violence and bloodshed. Sometimes individuals would illegally seize power and rule without respect for the old laws. These people became known as tyrants.

- **Some tyrants** were aristocrats who crushed the hopes of poorer people. Others were poor men who smashed the power of the aristocrats.

▼ *Draco and Solon were both lawgivers in Athens. Draco drew up his laws in around 620 BC, to impose order on the city. Solon reformed the laws in about 560 BC, once order had been restored. Most of Solon's punishments are less severe than Draco's.*

CRIME	DRACO'S PUNISHMENT	SOLON'S PUNISHMENT
MURDER	DEATH	DEATH
BANKRUPTCY	SLAVERY	GRADUAL PAYMENT OF DEBT
SACRILEGE – EXTREME DISRESPECT FOR SOMETHING SACRED	DEATH	NO PUNISHMENT
REFUSAL TO JOIN THE ARMY	DEATH	BRANDING WITH HOT IRONS
BREAKING A CONTRACT	DEATH	MONEY FINE
PERSISTENT DRUNKENNESS	DEATH	BANNED FROM PUBLIC OFFICE

Colonies overseas

- **During the Dark Age** and the time of the tyrants and lawgivers, Greece's population grew, which led to economic problems in some places.

- **The governments** of many cities decided to solve the population problem by planting colonies – founding new cities outside Greece.

- **Some colonies** were founded as a result of political disputes. The losers of the dispute would be told to leave on ships and found a colony.

- **In about 680** BC, the pharaoh of Egypt asked Greek merchants to establish a colony near the mouth of the River Nile. The resulting settlement was called Naukratis, and became one of the richest cities in Egypt.

- **New colonies** were independent of their parent cities, but most maintained strong links by way of trade and friendship that lasted for generations.

- **Corinth founded** the colonies of Korkyra, Corfu and Syracuse, Sicily. Massalia (now Marseilles), in France, was founded by colonists from Phocea.

▼ *A Greek temple at Syracuse, Sicily. Greek colonies on Sicily were very wealthy.*

- **The coasts** of Sicily and southern Italy were favoured for colonies between 800 and 600 BC, as the land and climate were similar to those of Greece.

- **Between 700 and 500** BC, many colonies were founded around the coasts of the Black Sea. At the same time, other colonies were founded in the western Mediterranean in what is now France and Spain.

- **Some colonies** became wealthy. Sybaris in Italy, was situated on a very fertile plain, and as a result rose quickly in power and opulence.

The power of Persia

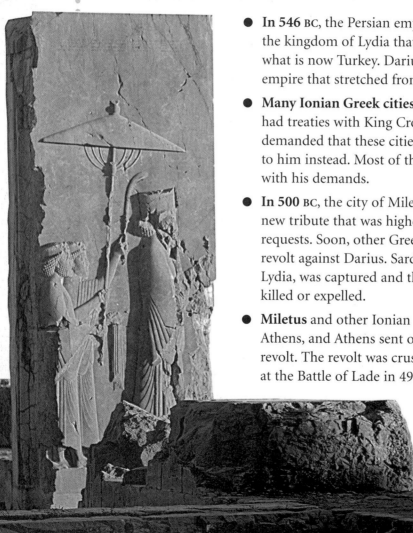

- **In 546 BC**, the Persian emperor Darius crushed the kingdom of Lydia that had ruled most of what is now Turkey. Darius already ruled a vast empire that stretched from Egypt to India.

- **Many Ionian Greek cities** had paid tribute or had treaties with King Croesus of Lydia. Darius demanded that these cities should pay tribute to him instead. Most of the cities complied with his demands.

- **In 500 BC**, the city of Miletus refused to pay a new tribute that was higher than the original requests. Soon, other Greek cities joined the revolt against Darius. Sardis, the capital of Lydia, was captured and the Persians were killed or expelled.

- **Miletus** and other Ionian cities were colonies of Athens, and Athens sent out a fleet to help the revolt. The revolt was crushed by the Persians at the Battle of Lade in 494 BC.

◀ *Rich carvings adorned the walls at Persepolis – the great city and palace of Darius' reign.*

- **Darius was determined** to punish Athens for aiding the Ionian revolt. In 490 BC, he sent a fleet and an army to attack Athens.

- **The Persian fleet** sailed first to the cities of Karystos and Eretria on the island of Euboia, which had also helped the revolt. Karystos and Eretria both surrendered. They were made to pay a heavy tribute, and the Persians burned down their temples.

- **The Persians then landed** at Marathon near Athens, with an army of over 20,000 men. They found the road to Athens blocked by an army of around 8000 Athenians.

- **The citizens of Sparta** promised to send an army to help Athens, but they could not do so until they had finished celebrating the religious festival of Carneia, during which no fighting was allowed. They said they would come in three days time.

- **When the Persian army** marched out of its camp, the Athenians launched a direct attack, hitting the Persians before they were properly in formation. The Persians were heavily defeated.

- **The Persians returned** to their ships and sailed back to the ports of the empire. The Spartans arrived in Athens the following day and congratulated the Athenians on their victory. Darius of Persia swore that he would have revenge on Athens and Sparta.

▶ *Darius, ruler of the Persian Empire, wanted to conquer Greece, but died before he could launch a major invasion.*

The Greek League

- **In 486 BC**, Darius, emperor of Persia, died. In 481 BC, his son Xerxes, began gathering a vast army.

- **Xerxes sent messengers** to every Greek state, demanding that they surrender and become part of the Persian Empire.

- **Sparta and Athens** announced that they would form a Greek League, made up of all of the cities that would agree to fight against Persia.

- **With an army** of about 200,000 men and a fleet of 700 warships, Xerxes arrived in northern Greece on 1 July 481 BC. The cities of Thessaly and Boeotia surrendered.

- **An army of 300 Spartans** and 6000 others, stood in the Pass of Thermopylae, a route through a narrow gap in the mountains, while the Greek fleet waited offshore in the narrow channel of the Euripus.

- **King Leonidas** of Sparta and the Athenian admiral Themistocles hoped that in the narrow space of the pass they could halt the Persian advance.

- **The Greeks held out** for three days. Then the Persians found another pass through the mountains, and King Leonidas and his Spartans were killed.

- **Xerxes captured Athens** and several other cities. After further advances he reached the Isthmus of Corinth, a narrow strip of land, surrounded by water on both sides, which was blocked by a new, larger Spartan army.

- **At the Battle of Salamis** (480 BC), the Greek fleet destroyed the much larger Persian fleet. Xerxes returned to Persia, and at the Battle of Plataea (479 BC) the Greeks defeated the rest of the Persian army that Xerxes had left behind.

- **The Persian Wars** continued for many years, but the Persians never again tried to invade Greece.

▼ *The Battle of Plataea, in which the Greek alliance defeated the invading army of the Persian ruler Xerxes.*

The might of Athens

- **After the Battle of Plataea** in 479 BC, the Greek league broke up. The Persian invasion had been defeated, and Sparta and some other states argued that the need for the league was over.

- **Some Greek states**, led by Athens, wanted the league to continue. They wanted to attack the Persian Empire and help the Ionian Greek cities break free from Persian rule.

- **In 477 BC**, representatives of the states wanting to continue the war met on the island of Delos. The meeting place was chosen because it was believed that Delos was an island sacred to the gods Apollo and Diana.

- **The states agreed** to form the Delian League with the objective of continuing the war against the Persian Empire. They asked the Athenian general and nobleman Aristeides to draw up rules for the league.

- **Aristeides was famous** for his honesty. He drew up a list that stated how much money each state had to pay to the league treasury to help fund the war.

- **The Persians** were driven out of the Aegean Sea in 476 BC. Ten years later the Delian League defeated the Persian fleet at the Battle of Eurymedon.

- **In 454 BC**, the treasury of the Delian League was moved to Athens by the Athenian politician Pericles. The power of Athens within the league began to increase, and Athens started to take money for its own use from the treasury.

- **Pericles and the Athenians** used the money of the Delian League to build beautiful new temples and strong walls to replace those destroyed by the Persians in 480 BC.

- **The peace treaty of Kallias** in 449 BC ended the war with the Persians, but the Athenians refused to disband the Delian League. Athens used its powerful fleet and army to defeat those that wanted to leave the league.

- **By the year 440** BC, the Delian League had fallen completely under Athenian control.

▼ *The Parthenon as it looked when it was first completed. The mighty temple was the crowning glory of Athens in the 5th century* BC.

The Peloponnesian War

- **The Peloponnesian War** began as a minor dispute between Corfu and Corinth, but it escalated rapidly after Athens interfered, and soon affected nearly all of Greece.

- **In 432 BC**, Korkyra failed to send a religious tribute to Corinth, its founding city. When Corinth sent ships to Corfu, the Korkyran fleet attacked and captured them.

- **Fearing the Corinthian response**, the Korkyrans sent ambassadors to Athens to ask for help. Led by the politician Pericles, the Athenians declared war against Corinth.

- **Sparta, Thebes and other cities** were worried about the growth of Athenian power, and did not want Corinth to fall to Athens. Sparta sent ambassadors to Athens to seek peace, but they were insulted and thrown out.

▶ *Although he was one of ten generals, Pericles was referred to as the leader because his military record commanded such respect.*

- **In May 431** BC, the Spartan army invaded Athenian territory.
  The Peloponnesian War had begun.

- **Most of the states** in the Peloponnese joined Sparta, as did the
  Boeoteian allies of Thebes. The forces of the Delian League fought on
  the side of Athens. Nearly every Greek state took sides and most joined
  the fighting.

- **The powerful armies** of Sparta and Thebes gradually gained a series of
  victories that gave them control of the land. The Athenian fleet and its
  allies gained control of the sea.

- **Athens tried to break** the stalemate by sending a fleet and army to
  capture Sicily in 413 BC. The expedition was a disaster and ended with
  the destruction of the Athenian fleet.

- **The Persians joined the war** on the side of Sparta. With Persian money
  and advisors, Sparta built a fleet of warships with which they blockaded
  Piraeus, the port of Athens. By 404 BC, Athens had run out of food and
  its people were starving. Athens surrendered to Sparta and Thebes and
  war ended.

The decline of Greece

- **Greece was exhausted** by the Peloponnesian War. Thousands had been killed, cities had been destroyed, and trade and farming had been disrupted.

▼ *The Delian League was formed under Athenian leadership to fight Persia, but soon became little more than an Athenian Empire.*

Epidamnus

THRACE

Byzantium

Stagira Thassos

Lampsacus

Abydus

Lemnos

PERSIAN EMPIRE

Aegean Sea

Lesbos

Chaeronea

Sardis

Thebes

IONIA

Plataea

ATTICA

Chios

Megara

Ionian Sea

Corinth Piraeus

Athens

Samos

Ephesus

Elis

Argos

Pylos

Sparta

Rhodos

KEY

Cythera

- neutral states
- ally of Athens
- the Spartan confederacy
- Athens and members of the Delian League

C R E T E

- **Under the peace treaty**, Athenian power dissolved. The states of the Delian League were given their independence, but Sparta insisted that politicians friendly to Athens had to be sent into exile.

- **The victorious** Spartans and Thebans used their new power to install governments that they could control in many of the smaller Greek states.

- **After 400** BC, the Spartans allowed the Athenians to run their own affairs, but only on the condition that they did not rebuild their powerful navy.

- **In 395** BC, the Athenians rebuilt the port of Piraeus. The Spartans decided that this broke the terms of the treaty, so they attacked and destroyed Piraeus again.

- **Thebes and Sparta** disagreed about how to divide the power in Greece. In 382 BC, the Spartans occupied Thebes, but were driven out in 379 BC. Warfare again spread across Greece causing more devastation.

- **At the Battle of Leuctra** in 371 BC, a vast army of Theban soldiers and their allies defeated King Cleombrotus of Sparta and his army. Cleombrotus was killed in the fighting.

- **Thebes disagreed** with her allies over how to divide the Peloponnese. A fresh war began that destroyed the power of Thebes.

- **Meanwhile**, the Kingdom of Macedonia to the north of Thessaly had been gradually expanding and growing in power. In 359 BC, Philip II became king of Macedonia.

- **Philip developed** new weapons and tactics for his army, conquering Thrace and Thessaly. At the Battle of Chaeronea in 338 BC, he crushed a joint Athenian-Theban army. Macedon now ruled Greece.

Alexander the Great

- **King Philip of Macedon** was assassinated in 336 BC and the throne passed to his 20-year-old son, Alexander. The new king at once announced that he would continue with his father's plans to rule Greece and invade the Persian Empire.

- **Thebes led a revolt** against Alexander in an attempt to free Greece from Macedonian rule. Alexander quickly captured Thebes and sold the entire population as slaves.

- **After the destruction** of Thebes, the other Greek states accepted Alexander's leadership and sent troops to join his army as it invaded the Persian Empire.

  - **In 334 BC**, Alexander marched into Persia with 35,000 men. At the Battle of the Granicus he defeated a local army, then marched on into the Persian Empire.

  - **At the Battle of Issus** in 333 BC, Alexander defeated Darius, emperor of Persia, and his army of around 100,000 men. He then marched south to occupy Syria, Palestine and Egypt.

  - **In Egypt**, Alexander founded the city of Alexandria and was declared to be a god by the priests of the supreme Egyptian god, Ammon.

◀ *Alexander the Great, king of Macedonia, is widely recognized as having been the greatest soldier in the ancient world.*

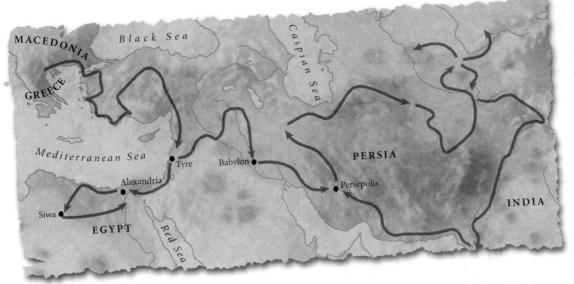

▲ *Alexander covered almost 32,000 km in the creation of his massive empire. His route is shown in red.*

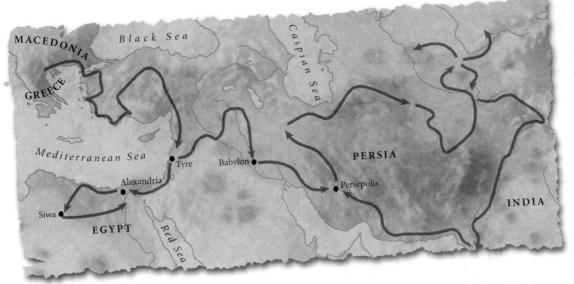

- **In 331 BC**, Alexander marched his army into Mesopotamia to face the main Persian army at the Battle of Gaugamela. Despite being outnumbered by about five to one, Alexander won the battle.

- **After capturing the cities** of Babylon and Persepolis, Alexander marched east to occupy the rest of the Persian Empire. He then invaded northern India, defeating King Porus at the Battle of Hydaspes in 326 BC.

- **Alexander turned back** to Babylon where he began the task of organizing a government for his conquests. He appointed Macedonian officers in government positions and told them to marry local wives.

- **At the age of just 32**, Alexander died in Babylon of a sudden fever. He is widely recognized as one of the finest military commanders of all time and is generally known as Alexander the Great.

The Hellenistic world

- **When Alexander the Great died** in 323 BC, his son Alexander was barely a year old. The Macedonian generals decided that Alexander's half-brother Antigonus should govern for the boy until he was old enough.

- **At once**, the generals divided up Alexander's vast empire between themselves, while claiming to rule the provinces on behalf of the infant Alexander.

- **Egypt and Palestine** were given to Ptolemy, Macedonia was taken by Antipater and Seleucus took control of Syria, Persia and the eastern provinces. Other smaller areas were grabbed by lesser generals.

- **Within five years**, the generals were at war with each other for the possession of disputed territories.

- **The generals appointed** Macedonians and Greeks to senior government and military positions in their territories. The Greek term for themselves was Hellenes, so this period is known as the Hellenistic Age.

- **The Hellenistic Kingdoms** introduced Greek language and culture across the Middle East. Local people adopted Greek ways of life.

- **As the power** of the Hellenistic Kingdoms declined, many countries made themselves independent. These included Pontus, Bithynia, Cilicia, Cappadocia, Galatia, Armenia and several of the Greek states.

- **In Egypt**, Ptolemy and his successors introduced new technologies that made Egypt one of the richest countries in the world. They continued to rule Egypt until 30 BC when Cleopatra VII was defeated by Rome.

- **The Seleucid Kingdom** gradually declined and by 65 BC it covered only part of Syria. The last king, Antiochus X, was deposed by the Roman general Pompey, who made Syria a Roman province.

◀ *The area of the world known to the Greeks around 200 BC. The rest of the world was thought to be inhabited by barbaric, uncivilized tribes.*

39

The Roman conquest

● **In 210 BC**, King Philip V of Macedon supported his ally, Carthage, by declaring war on Rome. Having defeated Carthage in 202 BC, the Romans decided to send their main army against Macedon. It was the first time a Roman army had fought in Greece.

▼ *Around 200 BC Greece was divided into a number of leagues (alliances) of cities. These gradually fell under the control of Rome, though some preserved a small amount of self-government.*

- **At the Battle of Cynoscephalae** in 197 BC, Philip of Macedon was defeated by the Romans under Quinctius Flamininus.

- **Flamininus forced Macedon** to give up control over the Greek cities and told the Greeks that they were independent once again.

- **Antiochus III**, ruler of the Seleucid Kingdom, went to war with Rome in 192 BC and persuaded some Greek states to join him. After Antiochus was defeated, the Romans disbanded the armies of those Greek states that fought for him.

- **Macedon was crushed** at the Battle of Pydna in 168 BC and divided into four provinces of the Roman Empire.

- **Roman forces** were sent through all the Greek states to arrest anyone who voiced support for Macedon. Several cities had their walls torn down and fines were imposed.

- **Sparta, Argos, Corinth** and other cities in the Peloponnese, formed an alliance. In 146 BC, Roman envoys attended a meeting of the alliance and made demands that led to a riot.

- **Rome at once declared war** against the alliance. Sparta and Argos were quickly overrun so only Corinth held out against the Roman commander Lucius Mummius.

- **When Mummius captured Corinth**, he ordered the execution of every adult male, and women and children were sold as slaves. All works of art were sent to Rome and the city was burnt to the ground.

- **After the fall of Corinth**, the Romans organized Greece into a number of provinces and made it part of their empire. The history of independence in ancient Greece was at an end.

Greece and the islands

- **Greece is a mountainous country** with few areas of flat, productive farming land suitable for growing good crops. Most farmland is along coastal plains.

- **The climate** of Greece is warm and dry with the occasional storm in summer, and mild, wet winters.

- **The warm weather** meant that the ancient Greeks spent much of their time outside. Political meetings were held in the open air, as were most religious and civic celebrations.

- **The Greek coastline** has numerous bays, inlets and peninsulas. These are home to many types of fish and shellfish that were harvested for food. The bays also provided ideal natural harbours.

- **The mountains** and the sea divide Greece into a number of regions. The land south of the Gulf of Corinth is known as the Peloponnese, the area around Athens is called Attica and the land around Thebes is referred to as Boeotia.

- **Greece has several groups** of islands. The Ionian Islands lie off the west coast of Greece, and the Sporades lie off the east. The Cyclades are southeast of Athens, with the Dodecanese lying further east of the Cyclades. The Aegean Islands lie in the Aegean Sea, east of the Sporades.

- **The plain of Thessaly** is the only large area of flat land in Greece. It covers about 7000 sq km, and is drained by the Pinios River that flows the northeast into the Aegean Sea.

- **Smaller areas of land** are named after their most important city. For instance, the area around Argos is called the Argive.

▼ *The coastline of Greece is heavily indented, and the mountainous terrain shown here is typical.*

- **Few people live** in the Pindos Mountains, which run north to south through the centre of northern Greece. The Mount Parnassos range lies south of the Pindos Mountains. The sacred Mount Olympos range lies in northeastern Greece.

- **The term** 'Greater Greece' was used in ancient times to refer to the colonies that lay to the west of Greece, mostly in Sicily and southern Italy.

Houses

- **In ancient Greek cities**, houses were built close together, and some even shared walls. City houses did not have gardens.

- **Houses were built** on foundations of stone. The walls were mostly built of sun-dried mud bricks, as they were cheap to make and easy to repair.

- **Most houses** had two storeys, though some were taller than this.

- **Roofs were made** by laying wooden timbers across the mud-brick walls at an angle to form a slope. The timbers were covered by a layer of twigs and dried reeds and pottery tiles were laid on top. The tiles were waterproof and the slope allowed rainwater to run off easily.

- **Every house** had its own front door, which opened onto the street.

- **The walls** that faced onto the street were plain, with only a few small windows. There were no obvious outward indications of how simple or luxurious a house was inside.

- **Most families** lived in houses with about 12 rooms. Poor people lived in houses that may have had just two rooms, while rich families might have had up to 30 rooms.

- **Houses were often built** around an open-air courtyard that was surfaced with cobblestones. Balconies ran around the courtyard on the upstairs level.

Bedrooms were upstairs

Slaves cooked in the kitchen

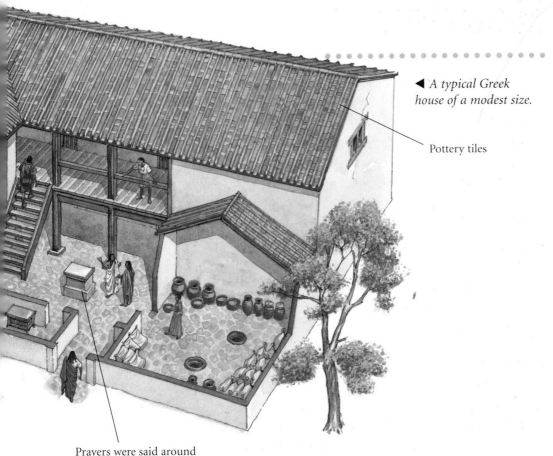

◀ A typical Greek house of a modest size.

Pottery tiles

Prayers were said around the altar each morning

- **The floors on ground level** were often tiled and sometimes had colourful mosaics. The floors of upper storeys were made of wood.

- **Most dining rooms** were brightly decorated, and were used to entertain friends and visitors.

City life

- **The streets** of most Greek cities were built in a grid pattern. This meant that they were straight and met at right angles. They were usually paved with cobblestones.

- **Most city streets** were wide enough to allow a cart to pass along it. The widest streets allowed two carts to pass going in opposite directions. Narrow alleyways just wide enough for a person to walk along ran behind houses.

- **Most cities** had a fortified hilltop site in, or near, the city centre. This was known as the *acropolis*, which means 'high town'.

- **The *acropolis*** was the area where important temples and public buildings were most commonly built.

- **There was usually** a large, open public space in the city called an *agora*. This was the market place where traders could meet to do business. It was also a place of assembly for the citizens.

- **All cities** had wells or fountains to provide water for their inhabitants. Wells drew their water from underground, beneath the city, while fountains spouted water that was brought along pipes from natural springs outside the city.

> ...FASCINATING FACT...
> Large storehouses were used to keep grain, olive oil and other foodstuffs.
> These were maintained by the government so that the citizens had
> enough food in the event of famine or a war.

▲ *Palace pithoi (storage vases) at Knossos, the chief centre of the Minoan civilization. A storage area in a Greek city relied on vases to store liquids and grains. Other objects were kept in stone-lined pits in the ground.*

- **Waste food**, human sewage and other rubbish was dumped in specially marked areas outside the city walls. Poor people carried their own waste in buckets, rich families had servants or slaves to do this work.

- **Strong defensive walls** surrounded every city. Even in peacetime, the city gates were closed at night to keep out wolves and bandits.

- **Public buildings** such as temples, theatres and courtrooms were usually built of stone. This showed how important they were as stone would last for many years longer than the mud-brick of private houses.

47

Furniture and pottery

- **Most furniture** was made of wood and fairly simple in design. The most common piece of furniture was a stool called a *diphros* that had four legs and a seat covered with leather.

- **The furniture of rich people** might have been carved with decorations, or inlaid with coloured woods, stone or ivory.

- **At mealtimes**, people lay on couches rather than sitting upright. Couches had four legs and were usually covered with a padded cloth mattress.

- **Cupboards and drawers** had not been invented, so most clothes and other objects were stored in wooden chests. Kitchen equipment and household tools were hung on hooks on the wall.

- **Only the rich had baths** because water was heavy to carry into the house. Most people washed using a wide, shallow bowl of water set on a wooden stand.

◀ *This detail from a painted amphora (a vase used for fermenting and storing wine) shows a table, stool and footstool.*

48

▶ *A black-figure vase from about 500 BC, probably made in Corinth. These pots were the finest ever produced in Greece.*

- **Greek pottery** was made from fine clay that was fired to produce objects that were practical for everyday use.

- **Pottery decorations** usually consisted of pictures or abstract patterns. The earliest pottery had black designs on a reddish background. After about 530 BC, potters learnt how to decorate pots with red figures drawn delicately onto a black background.

- **Wide, rounded pots** with two handles and a narrow neck were called *amphorae*. These were used to store food and drink for long periods of time, or for transport. These were the most numerous types of pot.

- **Drinking cups** were in the form of a wide, shallow bowl with two handles, set on a circular stand. Some people preferred large cups that could be passed around to share drinks.

- **The most impressive pots** were *kraters*. These were large upright vases decorated with elaborate pictures of gods or heroes. They were used at parties to store wine and water before it was served to guests.

Clothes and fashion

- **The warm Greek climate** meant that clothes were only necessary for warmth during the winter months. Most of the time the Greeks wore clothes only for modesty.

- **The cheapest fabric** was usually wool, which was woven into cloth at home. Linen was slightly more expensive but was much more comfortable to wear in hot weather. Only the richest people could afford to wear cotton or silk.

- **Men usually** dressed in tunics. These were made of two squares of fabric, which were fastened together at the shoulder and held in place at the waist with a leather belt.

▶ *Greek noblewomen dressed in* chitons. *The lady on the left also has a cloak.*

- **There were two types** of cloak for men. The *chlamys* was a square of cloth that was worn over one shoulder and reached to the knee. The larger *himation* was rectangular in shape and could cover the entire body to the ankles.

- **Sandals made of leather** were the most common footwear, although many poor people walked barefoot. In winter, leather ankle-length boots might have been worn.

- **Men tended to wear** their hair short and grow full beards. By the time of the Hellenistic period, men grew their hair longer and shaved off their beards.

- **Hats were made** of leather or wool. They usually had a low crown and a wide brim to provide protection from the summer sun.

- **Women often wore** a piece of clothing called a doric *chiton*. This consisted of two large squares of fabric, folded over at the top and joined by brooches at the shoulders. It was gathered at the waist by a cord.

- **After 500 BC**, the ionic *chiton* became fashionable for women. This consisted of two pieces of material about 1.6 m sq, that were sewn together down the sides and linked across the top, leaving a hole for the head. It was gathered around the waist or across the bust with straps and belts.

- **Women wore** their hair long, and tied it up with ribbons or scarves into a variety of styles.

Family life

- **The senior man** in a family was the head of the household. He was responsible for the actions of everyone in his family and other members of his family asked his advice before making decisions.

- **Most Greeks** lived in family groups that consisted of a married couple and their children. Sometimes, the parents of the married couple would also live in the same home.

- **The men worked** to support the family. It was considered a great humiliation if a man could not earn enough money to feed and clothe his family in accordance with his position in society.

- **When a baby was born**, the mother showed it to the father. If the baby was weak or sickly in some way, the father could refuse to accept it into the family and the baby would be left to die.

- **Until the age of about seven**, both girls and boys were brought up in the family home.

- **From the age of seven** onwards, children were prepared for adult life. Girls stayed at home to learn domestic skills from their mothers and boys went to school.

- **Children often stayed at home** with their parents until they got married, or could afford a home of their own.

- **Weddings were** usually arranged by the parents, although sometimes the views of the couple getting married were taken into account.

- **Weddings were celebrated** by the families of the couple. After sacrifices were made to the gods, the bride was led in a procession to the home of the groom. The couple then shared their first meal, at which point they became married.

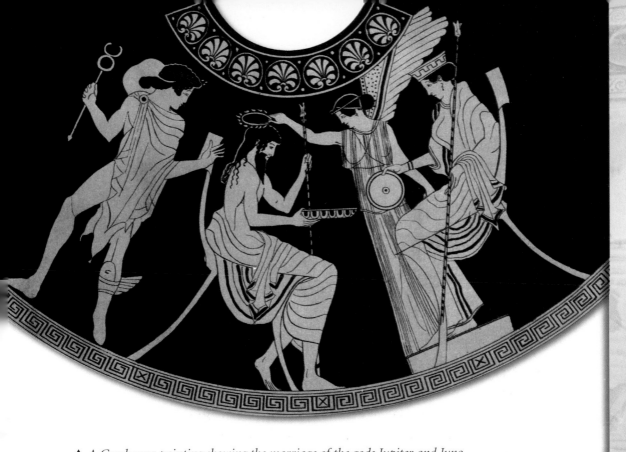

▲ *A Greek vase painting showing the marriage of the gods Jupiter and Juno.*
In ancient Greece, the bride and groom were married in their best clothes,
and crowned with wreaths of leaves.

...FASCINATING FACT...
Girls were considered to be adults from the age of 15, while boys
were not thought to reach adulthood until the age of 18.

53

Women in society

- **Women in ancient Greece** spent their entire lives under the protection and control of a male relative. At first, this was the woman's father, and after marriage, her husband. Widows remained under the protection of their eldest male relative.

- **The man who was responsible** for a woman was called her *kyrios*. The *kyrios* had complete control over any property owned by the woman and he could spend her money as he chose.

- **If a married woman** inherited property, her cousin or uncle could go to court to force her to divorce her husband. The inherited property would then go to her new *kyrios* – her cousin or uncle.

- **Women were not allowed** to own land or buildings. They were only allowed to own clothes, jewellery and personal slaves.

- **Women who were citizens** were not allowed to go outside of the city unless they were accompanied by a man. Many *kyrios* did not allow their women to walk about the city alone, either.

- **Most houses** had rooms that were reserved for women only. They were usually those at the back of the house, so that the women were hidden from visitors.

- **Special religious festivals** were reserved for female citizens only. At such times, women could gather without their *kyrios* being present.

- **Poor women** actually had more freedom than rich women. They had no slaves, so they had to shop for food and fetch water from the communal well themselves.

◄ *A vase painting showing a woman sitting outside on a folding stool. A pale complexion was thought to be a sign of nobility, so she holds a parasol to protect her skin from the sun.*

- **Domestic skills** such as spinning, weaving or cleaning were considered to be suitable occupations for rich women.

- **In Sparta**, women were allowed to own property, run farms or businesses and wander around the country freely. Other Greeks often used this as an example of how odd the Spartans were.

Education and schools

- **Boys attended school** from the age of seven. Schools charged fees that were paid by the father of the boy.

- **As soon as they had learnt the basic skills** such as reading and writing, boys from poorer families left school. From the age of 11 they helped their father at work, and learnt his trade.

▼ *A vase painting from around 500 BC illustrating the various lessons, such as music and writing, that were given at a school in Athens.*

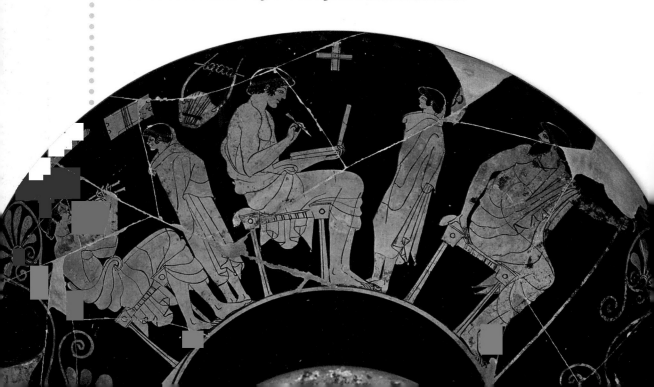

- **Boys from wealthy families** stayed at school until they were 18. They were escorted to and from school by a slave.

- **Education was divided** into three subjects, the most important being literature. Basic literature meant being taught to read and write, and being able to use grammar properly.

- **More advanced literature** involved reading famous books – especially the works of poets, such as Homer. Boys were also taught rhetoric – the ability to write and deliver good speeches.

- **Physical education** was the second subject. This involved learning to play different sports, as well as military training, which included practising using weapons.

- **Music** was the third subject. Boys were expected to learn how to play several musical instruments and to sing.

- **At the age of 18**, boys joined the state gymnasion. This was where philosophers, mathematicians and historians taught. There were no formal courses, so men could drop by as they pleased if they wanted to listen to a lecture or talk to a teacher.

- **Girls did not** attend school. From the age of seven, they were taught domestic skills, such as spinning and weaving, to prepare them to become good wives. Most girls were not taught how to read and write.

- **Education in Sparta** was different. Girls were taught how to read and write and they received an education similar to that of boys, although they did not take part in military training.

Leisure time

- **Most people** in ancient Greece worked longer hours than the average person today, so they had less time for leisure activities.

- **The centre** for most leisure activities was the gymnasion, which was often the largest and most ornately decorated building in a city. All adult men belonged to the gymnasion.

- **At the gymnasion**, men could listen to famous teachers, play sports or simply sit about and talk. Rich men went to the gymnasion every day, but poor men had to work long hours and may have gone only once in a month.

- **Rich men** would also attend the gymnasion to play music, sing and dance. By contrast, poorer men could use their musical skills to earn money by becoming professional musicians.

- **Board games** were a popular pastime in ancient Greece. One such game was played on a marked board that may have been rather like modern draughts. They also played dice games.

- **The Greeks** liked to hold dinner parties. Most houses had a dining room or *andron*, and at normal meal times the whole family ate there. In poorer houses, the *andron* might also be used as a bedroom. Some were richly decorated with mosaics and wall paintings.

- **Women and children** sat on stools or chairs, but men reclined on couches to eat. Food was served on low tables in front of them. Two or three men could share a couch.

- **Wealthy families** hired musicians and dancers to perform during dinner, while slaves served the food and drink.

▶ *A carving of a horse, probably from Athens. Riding and chariot racing were popular sports to watch, though only rich men could afford to take part.*

- **After the meal** was over, the women would leave the table. At this point the men would often hold a political or philosophical discussion called a *symposion*.

- **Some *symposions*** were less sophisticated affairs where men drank too much and played a game called *cottabos*, which involved flicking wine dregs from their cup at a chosen target.

Country life

- **In most Greek states**, about 20 percent of the population lived in the main city, and another 20 percent in other towns. However, the vast majority of the population lived in villages and on farms.

- **People who lived** in the country worked the land, growing crops and raising animals. Most farmers owned small farms, and the few that could afford larger areas of land hired servants or bought slaves to do the work.

- **The most important grain** crops were wheat and barley, which could only be grown on flat, fertile ground. Large plots of land were needed for grain crops as the ploughs needed room to work properly.

- **Smaller patches** of land were used to grow fruits and vegetables. These crops could be cared for by hand and so could be planted in the smallest plots of fertile land.

- **Grape vines** could grow on the worst soil and steepest slopes. Some grapes were eaten as fruit, but most were turned into wine.

Figs

▶ *Fruits were popular foods in Greece, and were eaten both fresh and dried. Some fruits were preserved by being sealed in jars filled with honey.*

Grapes

Pomegranate

● **Oxen were used** to pull carts and work machinery. These cattle were expensive so sometimes several farmers owned a pair jointly, or a farmer hired them from a more prosperous neighbour.

● **Olives were** an important crop. Like grape vines, olive trees can grow on poor soil and steep slopes. Olives were eaten, and were also crushed to produce olive oil.

● **Farmers kept some of their produce** for themselves to feed their families, and spare produce was taken to the nearest town or city to be sold at the *agora*.

● **People who lived on the coast** often worked as fishermen. They went out in small boats equipped with nets and spears to catch fish and other types of seafood.

● **If they were struck** by disease, or if there was not enough rain, the crops might fail. Famines sometimes killed thousands of people.

61

The farming year

- **The farming year** began in October, when fields that were going to be used to grow grain were ploughed.

- **Animals**, such as goats and sheep, were led up into the mountains in the autumn to graze. The winter rains produced lush grass on the slopes for the animals to eat.

- **The grain crops** grew during the winter months when the weather was mild and wet.

- **During the winter**, vines were pruned and shaped. The Greeks trained their vines along trestles set on poles so that they were just above head height. Vines began to grow around March.

- **Also in March**, farmers put large pottery vases upside down in their fields in the hope that wild bees would use them as their hives.

- **In April or May**, grain crops were harvested. The grain was cut with sickles and taken to the farm. There, it was threshed (separated from the straw) by being trampled by oxen or donkeys, and then winnowed (separated from the chaff) by being thrown into the air on windy days.

- **In May**, the shepherds brought their goats and sheep back down from the high mountains that were now too dry for grass to grow. The animals then grazed on lower slopes close to the farm.

- **Grapes were picked** in September. Men crushed the juice out of the grapes by stomping on them in large stone troughs. The juice could then be made into wine.

- **In October**, the olives were picked by shaking the tree branches with long wooden poles. Beehives were hung over smoky fires to drive off the bees, so the honey could be removed and packed into jars.

- **The farming year** began again in October when the fields needed to be ploughed.

◄ *Satyrs are mythological creatures known for their love of wine. Here they are shown engaged in a wine-making ceremony – picking grapes, crushing them with their feet and pouring the wine into jars.*

63

Food and drink

- **The basic food** of ancient Greece was grain. Wheat was usually ground into flour and then baked into bread. Barley was crushed and boiled to make porridge.

- **Meat was eaten** by rich people, or on special occasions. Roasted lamb was a favourite meat, but boiled mutton or goat might be served instead.

- **Sea fish** was eaten in quantity. Tuna, mackerel, snapper, octopus and squid were favourites. Sea urchins, mussels and clams were all considered to be delicacies.

- **Cucumbers, lettuces and onions** were used in salads, which were often served dressed with olive oil.

- **Vegetables eaten** included peas, artichokes, leeks, beans, turnips and carrots. These could be served raw and thinly sliced, but were more often boiled to make a thick broth.

- **Milk was not often drunk** as it would go sour in the hot weather quickly. Instead, it was made into cheeses, which could be stored for long periods of time.

◄ *Olive trees flourished in the dry, rocky terrain of ancient Greece, and oil made from the crushed fruit was used widely.*

- **Water was obtained** from natural springs. Wealthy people had spring water brought to their houses in large pots if there was not a spring nearby.

- **Greek wine** was heavy and sweet. It was stored in vats smeared with pine resin, which gave it a distinctive flavour. Wine was usually watered down before it was drunk.

- **The Spartan diet** was different. Men ate food thought to make them fit for battle. The main meal consisted of barley bread and vegetable broth, followed by cheese and figs.

▲ *The main course was followed by figs, grapes, cheese and nuts, such as almonds (above).*

. . . FASCINATING FACT . . .

An invitation to a Spartan military meal was considered an honour, but the food was so dull it caused one Athenian to remark, "Now I understand why the Spartans do not fear death."

Craftsmen

- **Greek craftsmen** produced goods made of pottery, metal, wood and leather that could then be sold for cash.

- **Early craftsmen** worked in their own homes, usually at the front of the house so that customers could easily do business with them without passing through the rest of the house.

- **Later craftsmen** set up shops to work in, which might have been on the ground floor of their house, or in a separate building.

- **Younger male relatives** would sometimes assist the craftsmen, learning the trade in the process. Slaves could be bought to help with non-skilled parts of the work.

  - **Some craftsmen** set up their relatives, or even a slave, in a business of their own. The craftsman would expect a share of any profits in return.

    - **One of the most important crafts** in ancient Greece was pottery manufacture. Greek pottery was of a high quality and was exported all over the known world.

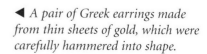

◄ *A pair of Greek earrings made from thin sheets of gold, which were carefully hammered into shape.*

◀ *A red figure vase carefully painted to show a warrior putting on his armour. Such exquisitely-made ornamental vases were very expensive.*

● **Some potters** were talented artists, able to decorate their pots with scenes from everyday life, or pictures of gods, goddesses and heroes.

● **Carpenters** produced furniture for houses, and handles for tools and weapons. Many were also employed to build houses, temples and public buildings.

● **Bronzesmiths** were highly regarded. They produced bronze helmets and other weapons in large quantities. Some specialized in making statues for temples and public buildings.

● **Blacksmiths** produced iron and steel used for making weapons or tools. Ancient Greeks could produce only small pieces of iron at a time, so it was used only for smaller objects.

Slaves and slavery

- **It is thought** that between one-quarter and one-third of the population of ancient Greece was made up of slaves.

- **Slaves had no rights** at all. They were regarded as 'living tools' for their masters. A master could order his slaves to do whatever he liked.

- **If a slave was injured** by someone, the perpetrator was expected to pay compensation. The money was not paid to the slave, but to the slave's owner, whose property had been damaged.

- **The poorest citizens** did not own slaves, but most families owned at least one slave to help them with their work or with domestic jobs, such as cooking and cleaning.

- **Rich families** might own up to 40 slaves. Male slaves were often employed as doorkeepers, while female slaves usually worked in the kitchen.

- **Some men bought slaves** to work in workshops. A man named Lysias (*c.* 440 BC–*c.* 380 BC), who lived in Athens, owned 120 slaves who worked in his shield business.

- **Slaves were expected** to stand aside to allow citizens to pass in the street and never to look a citizen in the eye. If a slave broke such rules he could be beaten.

- **People who had been captured** during a war were sometimes sold into slavery. It is also thought that some people sold their children as slaves to pay off heavy debts.

◀ *A plate decorated with a scene from a dinner party. A slave girl dances to amuse her master.*

● **Slaves were allowed** to own money and personal effects, but they were not allowed to own land or buildings. It was usual to pay a slave a small tip when you visited a friend's house.

● **Slaves could buy their freedom** if they managed to save up enough money, but only if their owner agreed to sell them. Sometimes slaves were freed when their master died.

Money and markets

- **Throughout ancient Greece**, people such as farmers and craftsmen made their living by trading.

- **At first**, people bartered their goods. This means that they would swap one thing for something else of a similar value. Bartering could be effective, but there was no easy way to compare prices.

- **By around 800** BC, some merchants began selling large quantities of goods for specified weights of gold or silver. Every time a deal was made the metal had to be weighed and verified for purity.

▼ *A modern-day market in Thessaloniki, northern Greece, where olives are being sold. Like the people of Greece today, the ancient Greeks tended to eat foods that had been locally produced.*

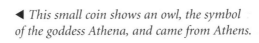

◀ *This small coin shows an owl, the symbol of the goddess Athena, and came from Athens.*

- **Around 630 BC**, the government of Lydia, in what is now Turkey, began issuing coins. The coins were made of gold and silver, and were stamped with a design that guaranteed the weight and purity of the metal.

- **By 570 BC**, most Greek states were making coins in gold and silver. By 540 BC, bronze coins for everyday use began to be issued.

- **As coining techniques developed**, coins were produced as circular flat objects, and their designs became more complex.

- **Dozens of different states** produced coins with their own designs. Athens had a picture of an owl, while Sybaris had a picture of a cow.

- **Most coins** were made to a standard weight and had standard names. Six bronze *obols* were worth the same as one silver *drachma*, 100 silver *drachmas* were worth the same as one silver *mina*, and 60 *minas* were worth the same as one gold *talent*.

- **Soon, nearly everything** was priced by how many coins it was worth. For example, an unskilled worker could expect to earn 3 bronze *obols* a day around 490 BC.

- **By around 300 BC**, there were banks that would lend and borrow money in exchange for interest payments. Greece had adopted an economy standardized by money.

71

Trade and merchants

- **Merchants earned a living** by buying and selling goods. They might buy pottery in Athens, take it to Sicily and sell it in exchange for wheat that they would then take back to sell in Athens.

- **Merchants relied** on the fact that goods could be bought for less money in one place, and sold for more somewhere else. For example, grain could be bought cheaply in Syracuse because of its large, productive farming system, but it was much more expensive in Athens because there was a lack of good farming land.

- **Before trade became common**, all Greek communities were self-sufficient, each producing all the food and goods necessary for its own survival. Farmers provided a full range of food crops, and craftsmen of every type lived within a city.

- **As trade became more common**, people began to specialize, producing a smaller variety of goods and concentrating on quality. For example, Athens was close to good clay, so its craftsmen could make quality pottery at reasonable cost.

◀ *A pair of gold rings decorated with lapis lazuli, a semi-precious stone. The gold came from local sources, but the beautiful blue stone was imported from Afghanistan.*

▶ *Greek coins were made from precious metals such as gold or silver. The design on this coin shows the head of Alexander the Great.*

- **Soon the people of Athens** were producing vast quantities of pottery that they then exported. In return, the Athenians were able to import food that they were not able to grow on the local poor soils.

- **Coins made trading** much easier, allowing merchants to carry a small bag instead of bulky goods. It also made it easier to compare prices of goods in different cities and countries.

- **Some merchants** became incredibly wealthy, but most earned a reasonable living that was only marginally better than that of a farmer or a bronzesmith.

- **The status of merchants** in ancient Greek society was not very high. Aristocrats and politicians preferred to earn their money by owning farms or renting out houses. Haggling over prices was not thought to be very dignified.

- **Some cities** had special areas of the *agora* where merchants from other cities were allowed to trade.

- **Merchants had to pay taxes** before they were allowed to bring goods into a state to sell them. Some cities grew very rich on these taxes.

Travel and exploration

- **Most Greeks** did not travel much. They visited the main city of their state and may have journeyed to a neighbouring state, but few people ventured much further.

- **Travel was expensive.** Time spent travelling meant a loss of income. Only men who could afford to hire others to do their work in their absence could afford to be away for any length of time.

- **Most people travelled** on foot over land, sometimes carrying a stick for support and a folding stool to sit on when resting. Rich men could afford to ride a horse or travel in a chariot.

◀ *A Greek merchant ship from about 400 BC. Ships such as these could only travel downwind, so crews sometimes had to wait weeks for a favourable wind.*

...FASCINATING FACT...

Around 350 BC, Pytheas, a Greek merchant from Marseilles, sailed around Britain. He then sailed further north to an island he called Thule (thought to be Iceland). No other Greek had ever travelled this far from Greece.

- **Men serving** in the army or navy might travel long distances to attack enemies or to help friends. Many young men got to see foreign places in this way.

- **Travelling was part** of a merchant's job. Merchants trading overland used donkeys or mules to carry goods because most roads were too narrow or bumpy for carts.

- **Most merchants** preferred to trade by sea. They used ships that were about 15 m long and 4 m wide. They were powered by a single square sail, although some larger ships had two masts.

- **Merchants only sailed** in the summer months, as winter storms could blow up without warning to make sailing dangerous.

- **Around 1000** BC, Greeks only knew about the eastern Mediterranean Sea, but by 700 BC, they were trading throughout the entire Mediterranean and the Black Sea.

- **After about 500** BC, Greeks began to sail beyond Gibraltar, which they called the Pillars of Heracles, to trade with the people of western Spain, western France and northwestern Africa.

Heroes in chariots

- **During the Mycenaean Period** of about 1800–1150 BC, warfare was carried out by kings and their bands of professional warriors. Only rich men could afford the expensive weaponry needed for warfare.

▼ *A scene from the 2004 movie* Troy *(Warner Bros. Pictures). Chariots carrying the heroes advance in front of the main army.*

- **The richest nobles** fought from chariots. These were two-wheeled vehicles pulled by two ponies, which could carry a driver and a warrior into battle. The warrior had throwing javelins and a sword.

- **Armour was made** of bronze. Horizontal bands of shaped bronze covered the body from the neck to the knees, while hinged plates covered the shoulders and upper arms. Famous warriors could be recognized at a distance by their armour.

- **Helmets were often made** from sheets of bronze held together by leather straps. Some were made of boar tusks stitched on to a leather cap.

- **Leading noblemen** often challenged each other to single combat before a battle. They began by throwing javelins, then they would rush at each other to fight with swords at close quarters.

- **Noblemen who won** a single combat fight sometimes celebrated by tying the body of their opponent to the back of their chariot and dragging it around the battlefield.

- **Some noblemen** led groups of elite warriors into battle. If the leading nobleman was killed, the warriors would flee the battle.

- **Most ordinary warriors** did not wear metal armour. Instead, they used large shields that were up to 1.8 m tall and shaped like a figure-of-eight. Their main weapon was a heavy spear.

- **Warriors fought** in groups with their shields overlapping.

- **Some places**, such as Knossos, Crete, could put hundreds of chariots onto the battlefield. It is likely that all warriors from Knossos fought from chariots instead of on foot.

Walls and citadels

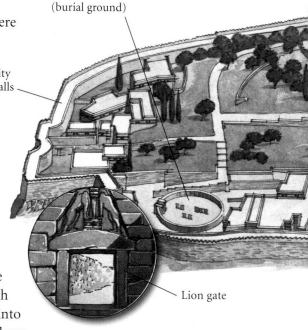

Grave circle (burial ground)

City walls

Lion gate

- **The cities** of Mycenaean Greece were surrounded by tall, sturdy walls built of stone. These were for defence against attacking armies.

- **The most famous walls** were those of the citadel at Tiryns in the northeast Peloponnese, which was home to the mythical hero Heracles. The walls were said to be so tall and thick that they could never be breached.

- **During this period**, city walls were built out of massive blocks of rough stone, with smaller stones pushed into the gaps between them. They may have been covered with plaster, and painted.

- **The most vulnerable parts** of these city walls were the gateways. These were often protected by tall walls and flanking towers. The gate at Mycenae had a huge sculpture of two lions placed above it.

- **The city of Thebes** had seven gates. According to ancient legends, seven heroes tried to break into Thebes by each attacking one of the gates. Six heroes were killed in the following fight.

Royal palace   Store rooms for food

◀ *A view of the stone citadel at Mycenae in about 1400 BC. Its strong walls would have been incredibly difficult to breach.*

● **The Greek hero Achilles** tried to win the Trojan War by smashing through a gate in Troy at the head of his personal guard. He was killed, it is said, by an arrow to his heel shot from the walls.

● **If the city fell** to assault, it was then pillaged and destroyed. Men were killed, women and children sold into slavery and all valuables were stolen from the city.

● **If the attackers failed** to break through the gateway, they would lay siege to a city. The attacking army camped outside the walls and fought a series of battles against the men from within the city.

● **The siege** would usually come to an end after a few weeks. Either the city government would offer tribute or land to the attacker if they went home, or the attackers would cease the siege and leave.

...FASCINATING FACT...
Some wars continued for years. Each year an army would attack a city only to give up and go home again. The siege of Troy was said to have lasted for ten years in total.

79

War aims

- **Some wars** in ancient Greece were little more than raids or skirmishes, while others were fought with the full resources of both sides.

- **During the Mycenaean Period**, kings often waged wars against each other to force payments of tributes, or to avenge insults.

- **In 743 BC**, a war broke out between Sparta and Messena over who had the right to use a temple that stood on the border between them.

- **Around 650 BC**, Athens fought a war against Megara for control of the island of Salamis, which lay halfway between the two cities. Most wars between cities were fought to settle territorial disputes.

- **In the 530s BC**, Athens attacked Naxos so that the tyrant of Athens could appoint his friend to be tyrant of Naxos.

- **During the period** of hoplite warfare, a general's main aim was to get a quick result. Armies were made up of unpaid citizens, who could not afford to be away from their farms and businesses for very long.

- **Both sides usually agreed** on a time and place for the battle. The rival hoplite armies would get in formation and then battle would begin.

- **If one side refused** to fight, the other would invade. The side being attacked would then either have to agree to battle, or ask for peace terms.

...FASCINATING FACT...
It has been estimated that in a typical hoplite battle, the winners would lose about 10 percent of their men, while the losers might take up to 30 percent casualties.

● **When the battle was over**, representatives of the two sides would meet to discuss a peace treaty. The winning side was expected to suggest terms based on the original dispute, and that the loser could accept.

▼ *An army of hoplite soldiers advances. Retaining strict formation was essential to achieving victory.*

81

Early hoplites

- **Warfare in ancient Greece** underwent dramatic changes between about 800 and 700 BC. From being dominated by noblemen on chariots and sieges of cities, an entirely new style of fighting developed.

- **The new style** of fighting depended on armoured men called hoplites, fighting in a formation called a *phalanx*.

- **The purpose** of the *phalanx* formation was to defeat the chariots of the noblemen. Chariots were very effective when used to attack other chariots, or when charging infantry in the sort of loose formation used in Mycenaean times.

▶ *A Corinthian-style helmet. These were hammered out of a single sheet of bronze, which made them extremely strong.*

- **In the *phalanx* formation**, rows of infantry soldiers stood very close together with their shields overlapping. This exploited the fact that horses will not run straight into a large solid object. They will shy off at the last minute and turn aside.

- **Horses would not charge** at men on foot standing close enough together to look as if they are a large, solid object, so the *phalanx* adopted this formation. The chariots of the noblemen soon became useless when confronted by a solid line of men.

- **At first**, the men were equipped in a similar fashion to the Myceanaeans. They had large shields, two throwing spears and a sword.

- **Around 750 BC**, the city of Argos introduced a new type of shield. This was round, about one metre across and made of layers of laminated wood fronted by a thin sheet of bronze.

- **The Argive shield** was lighter to use in battle, but still large enough to protect both the man who carried it and the man to his left. Soon, all the armies in Greece were using the Argive shield.

- **The throwing spears** were replaced in about 730 BC by a single 2-m-long thrusting spear with a large, heavy spearhead.

...FASCINATING FACT...
At first, men still carried swords, but in later years these were abandoned by all but the most professional soldiers.

Peltasts

- **Every adult citizen** was expected to serve in the army when ordered to do so during wartime. However, the poorer citizens could not afford to buy the heavy armour needed to be a hoplite. These men served as peltasts instead.

- **Peltasts were a type of soldier** named for the type of shield they carried, the *pelta*. This was about 50 cm across and was made of wickerwork covered with leather or linen.

- **The weapons** of the peltasts varied. Most carried a number of lightweight throwing javelins that were about 1.2 m in length. Each man might have carried up to ten javelins when on campaign.

- **Other light infantry** used slings. These shot a lead pellet that weighed about 50 g. A skilled slinger could send a pellet up to 100 m. A pellet could break the bones of an unarmoured man, and even stun a man wearing a helmet.

- **Few Greek soldiers** used the bow and arrow. Greek bows were relatively weak, shooting an arrow only about 150 m. Only the men of Crete were skilled in archery.

- **No armour** was worn by the peltasts because they could not afford it. This meant that they could not fight in the *phalanx*. Instead, they developed their own methods of fighting.

- **In battle**, the peltasts assembled in loose groups of about 100 men. They would run forwards to throw spears or slingshot at the enemy army as it advanced.

◀ *The peltasts were lightly armoured and carried several light throwing javelins into battle.*

● **Once they had thrown** their weapons, the peltasts would retreat, as they were no match for the hoplites in close combat. They would stand back at the rear to watch the clash between the main forces of hoplites.

● **After the hoplite battle**, the peltasts might be brought in to pursue a defeated army. They were also sometimes used by the losing side to delay the winning army from chasing the fugitives.

● **Peltasts were also used** to scout out enemy positions and to search the countryside for food and other items that could be used by an army.

85

Cavalry and horses

- **Horses were expensive** in ancient Greece. Only the richest men could afford to use their land to grow fodder for horses. It was far more profitable to grow grain crops to sell.

- **Noblemen sometimes chose** to ride their horses on campaign, but they usually dismounted when it was time to fight in a battle. The horses were sent to safety in the care of a slave.

- **Senior commanders** sometimes rode horses in battle. The extra height meant that they had a better view of the enemy's movements, and allowed them to move quickly from one part of the battle to another to issue orders.

- **Mounted men** were also used on campaigns to carry messages from their army back home, or between different parts of the same army.

- **Cavalry were** used as scouts, riding ahead of the army to watch out for the enemy and to guard against ambushes.

- **Mounted scouts** wore a helmet and carried shields similar to those of the hoplites. They were armed with javelins and swords to be used in the event of a meeting with enemy troops, but were not generally expected to fight.

- **It has been estimated** that a Greek city army of about 10,000 men might have less than 30 men riding horses on campaign.

- **The exception** was Thessaly. The land on the open plains was too damp for growing grain crops, but provided good grazing land for horses.

- **Thessalian cavalry** would gallop forwards towards an enemy *phalanx*. Seconds before collision, the horsemen would throw javelins at the enemy and then retreat.

● **Other Greeks** feared the Thessalian cavalry in battle, but the Thessalians rarely took their horses far from home because unfamiliar land might not provide enough food to sustain their animals.

◀ *Greek cavalry were rarely seen on the battlefield as only the richest men could afford horses.*

Hoplite armour

- **By about 600 BC**, the equipment used by hoplites had become standardized across Greece. All hoplites carried a spear and shield.

- **A hoplite's body** was protected by a *cuirass*. This was made of two sheets of bronze, one positioned at the front and one at the back. They were joined by leather straps or metal pins at the shoulders and down the sides.

- **In 600 BC** the *cuirass* was shaped to fit the body from shoulder to waist, and then flared out over the hips. Modern historians call this the bell *cuirass* because of its shape.

◄ *Later hoplites had a leather skirt hanging from their shield to protect their thighs against arrows and javelins.*

- **By 450 BC**, most hoplites wore a new type of *cuirass*. This consisted of 12 or 14 layers of thick linen, glued together. It was made in four separate pieces, one at the back, one at the front and two positioned over the shoulders.

- **The linen *cuirass*** was lighter and more comfortable than the bell *cuirass*. It was often strengthened by having small, overlapping pieces of metal sewn on to the vulnerable shoulder and upper chest areas.

- **Senior officers** continued to wear a metal *cuirass*, and by 400 BC this was elaborately shaped to resemble the muscles of a naked man. This style is known as the muscled *cuirass* and it remained in use for centuries.

- **The piece of armour worn** to protect the lower leg was called a 'greave'. Greaves were from sheet bronze and were worn below the knees to cover the area left unprotected by the shield. The greaves were shaped so that they clipped around the shin.

- **After about 450 BC**, only the men at the front of a *phalanx* were equipped with greaves, as only they were exposed to enemy javelins and slingshot. Some men began to wear armoured sandals to protect their feet as well.

- **The early** Corinthian-style helmet was made of a single sheet of bronze hammered into a shape that covered the entire head, leaving a T-shaped slot for the eyes and mouth.

- **A cheaper type** of helmet that did not restrict hearing and vision as much was the Chalcidian, which came into use around 400 BC. This had a round skull section with hinged cheek and neck flaps.

The phalanx

- **The key tactical formation** of the ancient Greeks was the *phalanx*. This formation was made up of armoured hoplite infantry men and could be adapted to include as many men as the army contained.

- **Each city** had its own variation on *phalanx* formations and manoeuvres, but the basic unit was the *lochos*, made up of 144 hoplites, divided into four *enomotia* of 36 men each.

- **On the march**, each *enomotia* was formed three abreast and 12 deep. The commanding officer, the *enomotarch*, led the right-hand file of men. His second in command was at the rear of the left hand file.

- **The front *enomotia*** was commanded by the man who led the entire *lochos*. This man had the rank of *lochagos*.

- **To form a *phalanx*,** the four *enomotia* assembled side by side. This produced a formation 12 men deep and 12 men wide. If the formation needed to cover a wider frontage, it would rearrange to six men deep and 24 men wide.

- **The front four ranks** of men held their spears overhead, pointing forwards over the tops of their shields. The rear ranks held their spears upright.

- **At the start of a battle**, the men would sing war songs and march into position. Then they would march towards the enemy.

- **When the two *phalanxes*** were about 100 m apart, the men would run forwards, keeping in formation. The two phalanxes would crash together when they met.

- **The men at the front** would use their spears, while the men at the back pushed forward with their shields. If a man fell in battle, the man behind stepped forward to take his place.

- **Eventually**, one *phalanx* would begin to give way. Once this happened, the *phalanx* would break up and the men would fall back quickly.

◀ *Most Greek battles involved rival* phalanxes *fighting each other at close quarters.*

Early warships

- **During Mycenaean times**, warships were not dissimilar to merchant ships, but they had oars so they could travel even if there was no wind.

- **When Mycenaean warships met**, the crews would first throw spears at the rival ship. When the ships manoeuvred closer to each other, the men would leap across to attack the enemy crew with swords.

- **One tactical aim** was to trap an enemy ship between two of your own. That way you would have twice as many men boarding the enemy as the enemy had to defend their own ship.

- **The *pentekonter*** was a new type of warship that was invented around the year 900 BC. Instead of boarding the enemy, the *pentekonter* crew would try to ram and sink the enemy ships.

- **Pine was the traditional material** used to make a *pentekonter*, and spruce was used for the oars. The strength of the ship came from three timbers that ran the length of the ship. The planks that formed the hull were attached to these timbers with wooden pegs.

- **A *pentekonter*** was about 20 m long and just 1.2 m wide. It was powered by 50 men rowing, arranged in 25 pairs sitting side by side. Each man used an oar about 4 m long that was held in place by leather straps.

- **A narrow walkway** ran between the rowers, connecting two larger areas of deck at the front and back of the ship.

- **The captain stood** at the back of the deck, along with a man who steered the ship using two large paddles, one either side, and a drummer who beat out a rhythm to keep the men rowing in time.

▲ *In Mycenaean times,*
warships carried large crews.
If they successfully boarded an
enemy ship they would attack
the crew with swords.

- **Men armed with javelins** stood at the front of the ship, ready to
  hurl them at the oarsmen on enemy ships. This would slow the enemy
  down and make them vulnerable to attack.

- **At the front of the ship**, a long metal-covered spike, or ram, projected
  forwards about 2.5 m. This ram was able to smash through the flank of
  an enemy ship.

Later warships

- **A new type of warship**, the *bireme*, was invented around 700 BC. This ship had two banks of oarsmen on each side, sitting one above the other.

- **The *bireme*** had a greater number of men rowing for the size of the ship, so it was able to move faster than the *pentekonter*, giving it an advantage.

◀ *A modern replica of a Greek trireme shows how the three banks of oars were organized.*

- *Biremes* **often had a mast** and a sail to help the ship move quickly if the wind was in the right direction. They were not used during battle.

- **Around 550** BC, a new type of warship appeared – the *trireme*. It was very similar to the *bireme*, but it had an extra bank of oarsmen sitting above the existing two on lightweight benches that projected over the sides of the ship.

- **By 500** BC, all Greek navies were equipped with *triremes* as their main type of warship. A few *pentekonters* were kept for use as messengers and scouts.

- **A typical *trireme*** would be about 40 m long and 3 m wide, though the upper benches might increase the width to around 5.5 m.

- **The crew** included 170 oarsmen, arranged with 54 on the lower and middle banks, and 62 on the upper bank. There was also a captain, a steerer and a musician who kept time for the rowers. In addition, each vessel carried about 15 soldiers.

- **The *trireme*** could move faster than any other warship and so it was able to ram with greater force. The ram had an upright pole, or bulge, to stop it driving too far into an enemy ship.

- **The ram** was made of bronze-covered wood, and often shaped so that it had three sharp prongs facing forward just below the waterline.

- **Around 380** BC, ships were made wider so that more than one man could pull on each oar. A typical *quinqereme* had two banks of oars, with two men pulling on each lower oar and three men on each upper oar.

Naval warfare

- **The main aim** of the captain of a warship was to ram and sink the enemy ships. This was best achieved if a ship was attacked from the side, so naval tactics developed to achieve this.

- **Enemy fleets** were sometimes ambushed in coastal waters. At the Battle of Salamis in 480 BC, the Athenian ships hid behind a headland. When the Persians passed, the Athenians were able to attack from the side.

- **In open waters**, a fleet would move into a line, side-by-side. Commanders tried to get their ships to line up facing the enemy.

- **The periplus tactic** involved sending several ships to attack the exposed side of the ship on the extreme flank of the enemy. This was usually only possible if one fleet had more ships than the other.

- **In the diekplus tactic**, ships moved into a line, one behind the other. The first ship would turn just before it met the enemy fleet to bump one ship out of the way. This would open a gap for the second ship in line.

- **Once a diekplus** had opened a gap, the following ships could push into the gap to ram the enemy from the side or from behind. The diekplus could be carried out only by a fleet with faster ships than the enemy.

- **The kyklos tactic** involved arranging the fleet in a circle with the bows facing outwards. This tactic was used by smaller fleets so that they had no exposed flank for the enemy to attack.

> ...FASCINATING FACT...
> To avoid being captured as slaves, some crews ran their ships ashore,
> set fire to them and fled. In 490 BC, one Greek crew did this and had to
> walk over 400 km to get home to Athens.

- **The long, narrow *triremes*** were difficult to handle in rough weather. If a wind blew up during a battle the ships would be driven out of position.

- **If one side began to lose**, their ships would try to row away as quickly as possible. If they could not escape the ships could surrender, but the crews would probably be sold as slaves.

▼ *The chief aim of* triremes *and later warships was to ram the enemy ship and sink it.*

Siege warfare

- **In Mycenaean times**, siege warfare involved bombarding city gates with rocks and axes. The city walls were too tall and strong for the armies to break through with hand weapons.

- **Between 1000 and 450 BC**, the Greeks did not lay siege to cities. During this time, city defences were very strong and Greek armies were made up of part-time soldiers who were ill-equipped to fight a long, drawn-out battle.

- **After about 450 BC**, the Greeks began to learn siege tactics from their Persian enemies, and developed ideas of their own. At the same time, some armies were made up of full-time soldiers, so lengthy sieges were more practicable.

- **One new tactic** was to surround the city, cutting it off from any sources of food or supply. A large army was necessary to keep a good watch for anyone trying to bring supplies to the city.

- **In 429 BC**, a small Spartan army built a wall of brick and timber all the way around the city of Plataea to stop supplies getting into the city.

- **A battering ram** consisted of a bronze-tipped tree trunk suspended from a wooden cage on wheels. This could be swung repeatedly at the city walls to smash through them.

> ...FASCINATING FACT...
> An assault ramp consisting of earth packed between timber piles
> could be built against the city walls. This allowed troops to storm
> up and over the wall.

▶ *The catapult was first used in Greece around 400 BC. It was built of wood and used twisted strips of rawhide or sinew for power. It could hurl a stone or bolt about 600 m.*

- **Defenders could counter** a battering ram by shooting the men working it. Alternatively, they could lower large hooks over the walls, catch hold of the ram and pull upwards to overturn it.

- **During Hellenistic times**, siege techniques advanced rapidly as the kings fought for control of the rich cities in what had been the Persian Empire.

- **Hellenistic siege engines** included wooden towers up to 40 m in height, which allowed attackers to target men on the city walls. They also featured catapults that were able to hurl projectiles that could destroy buildings, armoured wooden huts containing ballistae (a powerful ancient crossbow that shot giant bolts), and many different devices for drilling and tunnelling.

Mercenaries

- **Men who fight** for a country other than their own in return for payment are known as mercenaries. They are usually hired to do a particular job, or for a specified period of time.

- **In ancient Greece**, the armies of most states were made up entirely of their own citizens. Mercenaries were only hired if they offered specialist skills that the state could not find among their own soldiers.

- **Many Thracians** fought as peltasts. Peltasts were hired by so many Greek states that it is thought that wars were sometimes fought with Thracians fighting on both sides.

◀ *Mercenaries were usually specialist soldiers, such as this slinger from the island of Rhodes.*

...FASCINATING FACT...

King Cleomenes III of Sparta hired mercenaries to fight Achaea, a state in western Greece, in 222 BC. When Cleomenes failed to pay their wages on time, the mercenaries left. Sparta lost the following battle at Sellasia.

- **The men of Crete** were famous as archers. Cretans were hired as mercenary archers by many states, but the Cretan rulers had to give permission first.

- **The slingers** from the island of Rhodes trained daily. Many were employed as mercenaries throughout the Greek world and their services were expensive.

- **Mercenaries were famed** for the greed and violence they displayed when looting enemy territory. Some commanders used the promise of looting as a way to persuade mercenaries to fight for them.

- **In 402 BC**, Prince Cyrus the Younger began a civil war against his brother Artaxerxes, Emperor of Persia. He hired 10,000 Greek hoplite mercenaries to face the light Persian infantry.

- **After Cyrus was killed** at the Battle of Cunaxa, the 10,000 Greek mercenaries had to fight their way through 1000 km of Persian territory to get home. The march took 215 days.

- **At the Battle of Granicus** in 334 BC, about 10,000 Greek mercenaries fought on the Persian side against Alexander the Great. Alexander saw this as treachery and had the mercenaries killed when he won the battle.

King Philip's army

- **Around the year 350** BC, King Philip of Macedon completely reformed the army of his kingdom.

- **With his improved equipment** and tactics Philip conquered Thrace and most of Greece, while his son, Alexander, defeated the Persian Empire.

- **The core** of the new Macedonian army was the *syntagma*, a unit of 256 infantry, which marched, camped and fought together as a compact unit.

- **All the men** in the Macedonian *syntagma* were equipped identically. The infantry were recruited from peasants, so the weapons and armour were supplied by the king.

- **Each man** wore a bronze helmet and carried a shield that was about 60 cm across and made of wood faced with leather. The men in the front ranks wore a bronze *cuirass* and bronze greaves, but the men to the rear wore linen *cuirasses*.

- **The key weapon** was the *sarissa*. This was a heavy pike up to 7 m in length, which had an iron spearhead and a heavy iron butt so that it balanced neatly at the rear.

- **The front five** or six ranks held their *sarissa* pointing horizontally forwards at waist height. This produced a solid hedge of long, iron-tipped spears that prevented their enemy from getting anywhere near them.

- **The men further back** held their *sarissas* sloping forwards over the heads of the men in front. This produced a dense cover that could break the impact of javelins and arrows.

- **In battle**, each *syntagma* formed a square that was 16 men deep and 16 men across. They were trained to march forwards, sideways and backwards as a group.

- **In 334 BC**, the Macedonian infantry consisted of 50 *syntagma* – about 13,000 men. There were also about 7000 infantry armed with javelins or slings, who were probably peltasts.

KEY
1 Helmet
2 Shield neckstrap
3 Shield
4 Hand
5 Sarissa (pike)

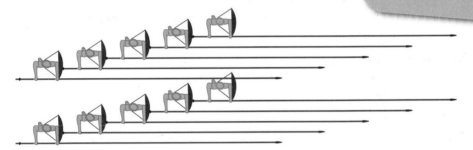

▲ *The 'closed order' position was used when the* syntagma *was advancing. The soldiers' shields had neckstraps because both hands were needed to support the* sarissa.

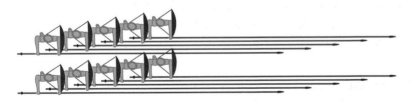

▲ *When the* syntagma *was on the defensive, the soldiers took on a 'locked' position, each one pushing his shield up against the man in front to provide a solid defensive wall.*

Companions on horseback

● **The success of the Macedonian army** on the battlefield was due to the careful combination of the *syntagma* with heavy cavalry, called Companions. While the *syntagma* held an enemy army, the Companions would charge through and sweep to victory.

● **The Companion cavalry** were recruited from noblemen and rich families. It is possible that each man may have paid for his own horse and equipment.

◀ *This Roman mosaic is thought to depict Alexander the Great's defeat of the Persian army at the Battle of Issus, in 333 BC. This detail shows King Darius in his chariot. His driver is desperately trying to turn as they face Alexander leading his cavalry.*

- **The armour consisted** of a bronze cuirass and bronze greaves, as well as flexible armour that protected the groin and thigh areas. No shields were carried.

- **The helmet** most commonly worn had a round crown with a flared brim that bent down over the ears. This was known as the Boeoetian helmet, and it gave good protection while still allowing excellent vision and hearing.

- **The main weapon** was a long, heavy spear, which was about 3 m in length. Each man also carried a heavy sword for use in case his spear broke in battle.

- **The cavalry fought** in formations known as *ilai*, which consisted of either 210 or 300 men.

- **When charging**, the cavalry formed a wedge shape, with the point facing toward the enemy. The impact of this formation when moving at speed was so immense that it could drive a hole through most infantry formations.

- **After the cavalry** had created a gap, other troops would pour through, then turn to attack the enemy from the flank and rear.

- **Alexander won** the battles of the Granicus, Issus and Gaugemala when he led his Companions in a charge that broke a gap in the Persian line.

- **The Macedonians** also had light cavalry called *prodromai*. These men wore no armour other than a helmet. They were used for scouting and for pursuing a retreating enemy.

War elephants

- **In 326 BC**, Alexander invaded India and fought the Battle of Hydaspes against King Porus. The Indian army included war elephants, and this so impressed Alexander that he started to use them in his own army.

- **Specially trained** Indian elephants were used in battle. They were controlled by riders who sat on their shoulders.

- **Each elephant** carried a wooden box on its back, held in position by strong chains. Inside the box crouched two archers and a man armed with a *sarissa*.

- **The archers** could use their high position to fire over the top of enemy defences. They also had a better view of enemy commanders or other high-value targets.

- **The man wielding the *sarissa*** was expected to drive off any enemy troops who attempted to attack the elephant. His armour was heavier than that of the archers.

- **War elephants** were trained to trample men underfoot, or kneel down and crush them with their tusks. They could also lift men in their trunks and throw them aside.

- **Siege work** required elephants that had been specially trained. They were equipped with metal plates on their foreheads with which they could push in the gates of a fortress.

> **...FASCINATING FACT...**
> Many horses were frightened of elephants, so a line of elephants
> would often stop a cavalry charge in its tracks.

- **Although they were difficult** to kill, javelins and heavy arrows could wound elephants badly. Wounded elephants were difficult to control and could inflict as many casualties on their own side as on the enemy.

- **Elephants could** be stopped by throwing planks studded with upward pointing nails on the ground, because these hurt their sensitive feet.

▼ *A scene from the 2007 movie 300 (Warner Bros. Pictures) showing a Persian war elephant in action. Elephants were powerful weapons, but could be unreliable.*

The end of an era

- **During the Hellenistic kingdoms**, the Macedonian style of warfare became prevalent. Kings recruited professional armies that could number up to 100,000 men.

- **By about 200 BC**, equipment had become heavier and more cumbersome. Heavy infantrymen wore shirts made of chain mail, and their shields were faced with bronze.

- **Elite infantry** were equipped with shields that were faced with highly polished silver or brass. In 220 BC, the Macedonian army had 5000 silver shield men.

- **For over a century** the Hellenistic monarchs fought mostly against each other. They refined the Macedonian tactics and weapons, and order and discipline became more important than flexible movement.

- **In 197 BC**, a Roman army invaded Macedonia. The Roman soldiers fought in smaller units called *maniples*, each about 160 men strong. Every man was equipped with a throwing spear and a stabbing sword, as well as a large shield.

- **At the Battle of Cynoscephalae** in 197 BC, the Romans launched an attack on the flank and rear of the Macedonians. The men of the *syntagma* could not turn quickly enough to get their *sarissas* to bear. The Romans defeated the Macedonians.

- **In 168 BC**, the Romans and Macedonians were again at war. King Perseus of Macedonia massed his entire army at Pydna. He took up a position where the Romans would be unable to get round his flank, as at Cynoscephalae.

- **The battle at Pydna began** with Macedonian success as the *phalanx* pushed forward. The long *sarissa* killed many Romans who could not fight back with their short swords.

- **The Roman commander** Aemilius Paullus then split his army up into individual *maniples*. These were ordered to push between the enemy spears and infiltrate the *phalanx*.

- **Suddenly**, the Macedonian formations collapsed. Greek-style fighting could no longer be counted on for success. It was the end of an era.

▶ *A Roman legionary of about 170 BC. The Roman equipment was no better than that of the Greeks, but Roman soldiers were better trained with more flexible tactics, which gave them the advantage.*

109

Kings and palaces

- **During the Mycenaean Period**, each city state was ruled by a king, and had several families of wealthy nobles.

- **Written records** from this period are rare, and those that have survived are usually lists of goods being stored or sold. Little is known for certain about the system of government during this period.

- **It is thought that the king** had total power over the city and its inhabitants, and could make laws and order punishments as he wished.

- **It is likely that the nobles** advised the king during councils, which were held to discuss important issues. However, it was the king who had the final say in any decision.

- **Kings often made alliances** with each other. Marriages between royal families were a common way to make an alliance more formal.

- **Every city** was dominated by a large palace where the king lived and worked. The palace also contained storerooms that housed food and other goods.

- **A king** would have kept all his valuables in the storerooms within his palace. Money had not yet been invented, so wealth was measured in terms of precious objects.

- **Laws were made by the kings**, who also acted as judges in legal disagreements. People brought their disputes before the king and he decided who was in the right and what punishment the lawbreaker should be given.

- **Part of a king's duty** was to be brave and successful in warfare. Kings had to protect their city and lands from other kings and their armies, and from raiders.

● **When a member of the royal family died**, they were buried in a large underground tomb filled with rich treasures. At Mycenae, the kings had gold masks placed over their faces before burial.

▼ *A section of the palace at Knossos on the island of Crete. A succession of powerful kings ruled a rich and populous kingdom here.*

The polis

- **The ancient Greeks** lived in separate communities, each usually based around a single city. A community such as this is known as a *polis*, translated as 'city-state'. The number of *poleis* in Greece varied, but usually numbered well over 100.

- ***Poleis* were independent** of each other The people of ancient Greece recognized that they all shared a common culture when compared to foreigners such as Persians or Romans, but they did not see themselves as part of a single nation.

- **The *polis*** was defined as a group of people living in a particular area, who ruled themselves and did not answer to any outside authority.

▼ *The Acropolis in Athens was the central part of the city-state. It was where elections were held and meetings took place.*

...FASCINATING FACT...

In 427 BC, the Spartans destroyed the *polis* of Plataea. The Plataean citizens that survived moved to Athens. More than 50 years later, Plataea was rebuilt and the citizens returned.

- **The centre of a *polis*** was usually a city. This was where the law courts and the most important temples were situated, and where the business of government was carried out.

- **The land** that a *polis* covered varied from largely barren and empty, or rich and dotted with farms and villages. Sometimes a *polis* would encompass more than one city.

- ***Poleis* ranged in size** from communities with only a few hundred citizens, to some with tens of thousands. They also varied widely in their wealth and culture.

- **Only adult men** were considered to be full citizens. Women and children from families that had citizen status still did not have the same rights as male citizens.

- **Not all *poleis*** were completely independent – some had to pay tribute to a more powerful *polis* nearby. Sometimes *poleis* would voluntarily join together to form a league or alliance.

- ***Poleis* that had joined together** would sometimes gradually lose their individuality. The territory of Attica contained several towns, but they all belonged to the *polis* of Athens.

Tribes

- **The Greek Dark Age** was characterized by invasions and migrations. Few records survived this period, but later traditions reveal much about the it.

- **Most of the people** who lived in Crete, the Peloponnese, and the islands of Rhodes, Kos, Samos and some others nearby, believed that they were descended from a tribe called the Dorians.

- **The inhabitants** of the islands of Lesbos, Lemnos, Thasos, Samothrace and the nearby mainland believed they were descended from the Aeolian tribe.

- **The people** of Attica, the Cyclades islands, Chios and the coast of modern western Turkey were descendants of the Ionian tribe.

- **The various** *poleis* of the different tribes often helped each other. For example, the 12 Ionian cities in Asia Minor (modern Turkey) frequently fought on the same side in wars.

- **The kingdom of Macedonia** lay just north of Mount Olympos. Although the Macedonians spoke a form of Greek and shared much of the Greek culture, the people of Greece did not think of the Macedonians as true Greeks.

- **Epirus lay to the northwest** of mainland Greece. The royal family there claimed to be descended from the hero Achilles and the people spoke a dialect of Greek. However most Greeks thought of the Epirots as uncivilized and did not associate themselves with them.

> ...FASCINATING FACT...
> At first the Greeks looked down on the Romans as barbarians. It was only after Rome conquered Greece that the Romans were accepted.

- **The Greeks** referred to all people from outside Greece as 'barbarians'. This word derives from the language of the Celts, which to Greek ears sounded as if the men were muttering 'bar-bar-bar'.

- **Barbarians were banned** from taking part in certain religious festivals and were not allowed to live in particular areas.

▶ *Greek architecture was recognized as a symbol of civilization, and was copied by other peoples, such as the Macedonians and Romans.*

The rule of nobles

- **By around 700 BC**, the usual form of government in most Greek *poleis* was oligarchy – a small group of people (the oligarchs) who ruled over everybody else.

- **In most Greek *poleis*,** the oligarchs were aristocrats or wealthy noblemen – powerful landowners.

- **The majority of the land** in a *polis* was owned by a relatively small number of men. This meant that most farmers did not actually own the land on which their farm was situated. Instead, they rented it from the landowners on a system known as share-cropping.

- **As payment** for the use of the land, a farmer had to give a share of his crop to the landowner. There was usually a minimum payment so that farmers could not cheat the landowners out of payment by claiming that they had only grown a small amount that year.

- **If a farmer** could not produce the amount of food or crops demanded by the landowner, he would fall further into debt.

- **The aristocratic landowner** could then ask the farmer to pay off his debt by doing jobs for him. These could involve taking part in a demonstration or even pressurizing a political rival.

- **If a farmer** fell deeply in debt, the landowner had the right to sell the man and his family as slaves.

- **Aristocrats did not** have to earn their livings, so they could devote their time to running the government.

- **Judges and lawyers** were usually educated aristocrats. They often made certain that the law favoured their fellow wealthy noblemen.

Spartan Constitutional System

c. 500 BC

King No.1 ——————— **King No.2**

Led the army, advised by the generals.

Led the government, advised by the Gerousia.

Generals

Up to ten men, elected by the Assembly, advised the king on campaign.

Gerousia

28 men aged over 60 elected by the Assembly. Advised the king and proposed new laws to the Assembly.

Hoplites

Selected by the Assembly, to either go on campaign or stay at home.

Ephors

Five men elected by the Assembly. Able to punish any king or member of the Gerousia who broke the law.

Assembly

All adult male citizens chose a new king when an old one died, declared war or peace, elected Ephors, Gerousia and Generals, and selected who would go on campaign and who would stay at home to guard Sparta.

▲ *Spartan citizens usually worked on state-owned plots of land. Citizens who could not make enough money to pay their taxes lost their land and their citizenship. Without citizenship, a Spartan could have not attend the Assembly and could have no influence in public life.*

● **The rule of the aristocrats** was never formalized and was based on wealth, influence and debts. Few poor people had any kind of say in how the *polis* was run.

The coming of the tyrants

- **Aristocrats ruled** without paying much attention to what the ordinary citizens wanted.

- **Aristocrats used their strength** on the battlefield to justify their authority. They argued that it was they who kept the *polis* safe from foreign attack, as aristocrats in chariots were the most powerful soldiers.

- **After about 750** BC, hoplites became the most powerful type of soldier in Greece, and many hoplites were ordinary citizens, rather than aristocrats.

- **As aristocrats became less important** in battle, their control over the government of the *polis* began to weaken.

- **In some cities**, aristocrats hired mercenaries to enforce their rule. In others, they simply ignored the growing concerns of the citizens.

- **Most government officials**, lawyers and judges were aristocrats, so they often passed new laws aimed at denying power to the citizens. These laws were rigorously enforced.

- **Some citizens** gradually came to believe that they would have to break the laws to take some political power away from the aristocrats.

FASCINATING FACT
Hoplites sometimes refused to march to war if they disagreed with the reasons why the aristocrats had declared war. This caused rioting to break out in some cities.

▲ *The ruins of one of the beautiful temples at Corinth. The tyrants of Corinth worked hard to ensure economic prosperity, making the city one of the richest in Greece.*

- **In ancient Greece**, the act of ruling a state without obeying the law was called tyranny. A man who ruled in this way was a tyrant.

- **The first known tyrant** was Kypselus of Corinth. He was a military commander who led an army of hoplites into Corinth, and the ruling aristocrats were killed or forced into exile. This marked the beginning of the rule of the tyrants.

119

The rule of the tyrants

- **The tyrant** Kypselus of Corinth took power with the backing of the hoplites of the citizen army. He proved to be very popular and was even able to go about Corinth unarmed and without a bodyguard.

- **Kypselus used the slogan** 'give justice to Corinth' throughout his rule. His first act to was ensure that all citizens were viewed as equal in the law courts – aristocrats and citizens were given the same punishments for the same crimes.

- **The key to Kypselus' success** was probably that he listened to the needs of ordinary citizens. It is thought that he called meetings of the citizens to discuss key decisions.

- **Kypselus was so popular** that when he died, his son, Periander, was immediately installed as the new tyrant of Corinth.

- **The city of Sicyon** appointed a tyrant called Orthagoras in 650 BC. He quickly gained a reputation for being honest and impartial, but he imposed severe penalties on anyone who broke his laws.

- **Orthagoras and his descendants** ruled as tyrants of Sicyon for more than 100 years.

- **The laws of Pittakos**, tyrant of the city of Mytilene on Lesbos, were biased against the aristocrats. For example, if an aristocrat committed a crime while drunk, he had to suffer double the penalty that anyone else would have been given.

- **Pittakos resigned his position** as tyrant in about 570 BC. He set up a constitution by which the citizens could elect government officials.

- **By about the year 500** BC, the rule of the Greek tyrants was ending. Most had either died, resigned or been ousted from power.

- **Tyrants continued to rule** in the Greek cities of Sicily and southern Italy after 500 BC.

Name	Details	Known for...
Peisistratos	Tyrant of Athens 560–527 BC	Patronizing the arts.
Gelon	Tyrant of Syracuse 491–475 BC	Defeating Carthage at the Battle of Himera (480 BC).
Hieronymos	Tyrant of Syracuse 216–211 BC	Patronizing science and employing Archimedes.
Anaxilaos	Tyrant of Rhegium d. 476 BC	Never executing anyone for any crime.
Phalaris	Tyrant of Agrigentum d. 552 BC	Building the Brass Bull of Sicily statue.
Phintias	Tyrant of Agrigentum d. 282 BC	Organizing the best parties in the world.

Lawgivers

- **Lawgivers were appointed** in some Greek states instead of tyrants. Lawgivers did not rule the state, but set up rules and constitutions that were designed to end disputes between aristocrats and citizens.

- **One problem in many states** was that it was the responsibility of the family of the victim to choose and enforce the appropriate punishment for the criminal.

- **Feuds developed** between different families and clans over arguments about legal punishments, and could become violent. Fighting in the streets was common and many men were killed as a result.

- **All lawgivers** sought to establish a method by which punishments could be decided and agreed upon by everyone. Some specified particular punishments for various common crimes, while others set up panels of judges to review each crime and give out appropriate punishments.

- **In some states**, the laws were not made public by the aristocrats. Lawgivers usually published their laws and decisions so that even the poorest knew what they were or were not allowed to do.

- **Getting into debt** was a common problem for the poorer people of ancient Greece. In some cities, men who had got into debt were sold as slaves, but this led to a decline in the numbers of citizens.

- **Slavery as a punishment for debt** was made illegal by most lawgivers. Instead, they introduced limits on how much interest a money lender could charge and set up different ways that a debt could be paid off.

- **Some of the laws** that were brought in by the lawgivers seem very strange to us today. In Athens, idleness was made a crime, so if a man did not have a job, he could be prosecuted in court and punished.

▲ *A modern reconstruction of the Stoa of Attalos in Athens. It was originally used as a market and meeting place, but is now a museum.*

- **Lawgivers also affected** the way states were run. In Athens, the lawgiver Solon established a council called the *boule* that ran the day-to-day affairs of government in Athens.

- **Not all Greek states** consulted a lawgiver. Some states continued to abide by traditional laws and ways of doing things.

The growth of democracy

● **The word democracy** is based on two words from ancient Greece. *Demos* means citizens who are not aristocrats, while *kratos* means power. Effectively the word democracy means 'people-power'.

▼ *Voting followed strict procedures, and varied from city to city. In Sparta, men raised their hands to vote, elsewhere they put coloured balls in pots.*

- **Both tyrants and lawgivers** sought to solve social problems by removing legal restrictions that the public objected to.

- **Democracy began to be seen** as a possible way to solve social and legal problems. If the ordinary people had some way to change laws and government policy, they would be less likely to cause trouble.

- **Solon, lawgiver to Athens**, began this process. He arranged that only aristocrats could serve as government officials, but that they had to be elected by the Assembly of all citizens.

- **When an official retired**, he could be appointed to join the *Areopagus*, a panel of judges, by his fellow aristocrats. This panel dealt with serious crimes, deciding if a person was guilty and what his punishment should be.

- **The Council** was a group of men elected by the Assembly. It decided how often the Assembly met and how votes were to be conducted. Aristocrats were not allowed to serve on the Council.

- **In 546 BC**, a rivalry between the citizens of Athens and the surrounding towns and the poor farmers living inland, led to a tyrant named Peisistratus taking power in Athens.

- **Peisistratus reformed** taxation laws but made few changes to the constitution of Solon.

- **After Peisistratus died**, Cleisthenes, a nobleman, used support in the Assembly to introduce radical new government structures that put even more powers into the hands of the ordinary citizens.

- **Cleisthenes set up new systems** for local and national government that allowed ordinary citizens more rights and power. For the first time, people began to talk about 'democracy'.

125

Archons and councils

- **Records of the government structures** of most Greek *poleis* have not survived, but it is accepted that the system in Athens was much admired, and parts of it were copied elsewhere.

- **In Athens**, the most important government officials were the nine archons, who were elected annually. The archons looked after law and order throughout the *polis*.

- **The most senior** was known as the Archon *Eponymous*. He dealt with disputes about inheritance, land ownership and the care of orphans. The second archon, the *Basileus*, dealt with disputes about religion.

- **The other archons** kept order in the streets. They hired men to arrest criminals and to make sure that everyone obeyed the laws of Athens.

- **Athens also had** ten *strategoi*. These men were also elected by the Assembly, but they were not necessarily aristocrats. At first, the *strategoi* were generals, each in command of one-tenth of the Athenian army.

- **Around 485 BC**, many powers were transferred from the archons to the *strategoi*, and many of the activities of the aristocratic archons became largely ceremonial.

- **Lesser officials** in the government looked after basic administration and the day-to-day business.

- **Before Cleisthenes**, the lesser officials were unpaid, so only wealthy aristocrats could afford to do these jobs. After Cleisthenes, they were paid a basic salary. Even the poorest citizen could then become a government official.

126

▲ *An Archon in Athens judges a dispute between two foreign merchants about a business deal. The Archons were aristocrats elected by the Assembly.*

● **The Council** that decided how the Assembly worked was elected at the start of every year. The *polis* was divided up into 500 areas, each of which elected one Council member.

● **By 480 BC**, a motion could be put to the Assembly only if the Council had first agreed to it. This gave the Council a great deal of power.

Assemblies and voting

- **Every adult male citizen** was a member of the Assembly in their *poleis*. The way the Assembly functioned varied from state to state.

- **Assemblies usually met** in the open air so that there was enough room for all citizens to attend. At Athens, the Assembly met on the slopes of a small hill called the Pnyx.

- **Under the rule** of the aristocrats, most Assemblies were summoned so that the nobles could announce their policies. Men at the Assembly could applaud, or not, to show approval, but they did not have the power to change the decisions.

▶ *In Athens, men wrote down the way they were voting on pieces of broken pottery called* ostraka, *and handed them in to the officials.*

The word 'ostracism' means 'broken pottery'. The vote got this name because people had to write their vote on a piece of broken pottery.

- **In some *poleis*,** Assemblies could vote on proposals put forward by the aristocrats. Assemblies could only approve or reject ideas, they could not come up with ideas themselves.

- **Votes were usually decided** by a show of hands. A formal vote would only be held if there was no clear majority.

- **One system of voting** was to give each man two clay discs. A disc with a hole in meant yes, one without a hole meant no. Each citizen dropped his chosen disc into a box to vote.

- **The vote** could be kept secret. If a citizen did not want anyone else to know which way he was voting, he could put his thumb over the centre of the clay disc to hide if there were a hole or not.

- **Tyrants often allowed Assemblies to vote** on proposals. Most tyrants wanted to be popular with the large number of poorer citizens, and allowing them to vote freely often ensured this.

- **In Athens,** the assembly voted once each year on ostracism. This meant that they voted to exile a person that they did not like from the *polis*. If anyone got enough votes they had to leave Athens for ten years.

Citizens and strangers

- **Only citizens** were able to take part in the government and public life of a *polis*. Being a citizen of a *polis* was considered a great a honour.

- **Citizens were usually men** aged over 18. In some states, men had to be over the age of 21, or had to have served in the army to be considered citizens.

- **At the time** of the aristocrats, a man could become a citizen by living in a city for a certain number of years, or by a decree from the government.

- **The right to citizenship** passed from a man to his sons, but did not pass through a woman to her children.

- **By about 400** BC, a boy could become an Athenian citizen only if his father was a citizen and his mother was the daughter of a citizen.

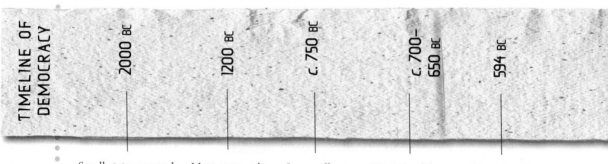

TIMELINE OF DEMOCRACY

2000 BC
Small states are each ruled by a king – some by force, others by consent. Most kings inherit power, but some seize it with armed men.

1200 BC
Most states rule by oligarchies – groups of noblemen who impose their rule on the state.

c. 750 BC
Sparta allows citizens to elect a new king when one dies, but they must choose from within the royal family.

c. 700–650 BC
Most Greek states allow all male citizens to vote in elections, but their power is usually limited.

594 BC
Solon gives the Athens assembly new powers. The word 'democracy', is coined.

- **People outside of this criteria** had to be given citizenship by a vote of the Assembly, which very rarely happened.

- **The children** of a citizen and an outsider, or foreigners who had come to live in the *polis*, were non-citizens. They were usually called freemen.

- **Men who were not citizens** were allowed to own property and enforce contracts on citizens. They were also protected by law against fraud and theft.

- **Non-citizens** could not attend the Assembly or appear in court. If they were involved in a legal dispute, they had to get a citizen to appear in court on their behalf.

- **Slaves had almost no rights** at all. A slave who gained his freedom could become a freeman, but he was never allowed to become a citizen.

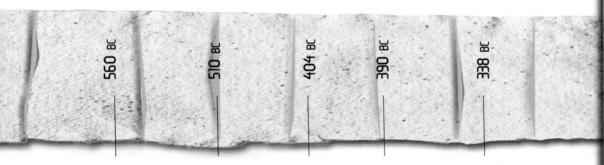

560 BC
Democracy overthrown in Athens by the tyrant Peisistratus to end a political deadlock between men from the city, and farmers.

510 BC
Democracy restored at Athens when Hippias, son of Peisistratus, is expelled.

404 BC
Athens loses the Peloponnesian War to Sparta. Sparta imposes rule on Athens and its allies.

390 BC
Democracy returns to Athens and many other cities after the defeat of Sparta.

338 BC
King Philip of Macedon defeats an alliance of Greek states at the Battle of Chaeronea. Greek independence and democracy ends.

The law

- **During the Mycenaean Period**, the word of a king was law. It is thought that there were no written laws at all, just customs and an agreed moral code that decreed some things, such as theft, to be wrong.

- **If one person** had a complaint against another, for instance that he had stolen something, the two people went to the king. The king then decided if a crime had been committed and, if so, what the punishment should be.

- **During the time of aristocratic rule**, the aristocrats acted as judges to decide whether or not someone was guilty and what their punishment should be. Some *poleis* had written laws, but these were not usually made public.

- **A key demand** of ordinary citizens in most cities was that laws should be stated publicly, so that everyone knew what they were and what the punishments for breaking them would be.

- **In Athens** and some other cities, a stone tablet was set up in the *agora* and was used to list the most important laws. New laws had to be announced in the *agora* and then a written copy was put up so everyone could read it.

- **Some cities had armed police** to arrest criminal suspects and take them to court. Other cities did not, and it was the citizen's responsibility to arrest anybody he thought had committed an offence against him.

- **In democratic systems** the judges were elected, usually by the Assembly, to serve for a fixed amount of time. If people thought a judge did not reach fair decisions, he was replaced.

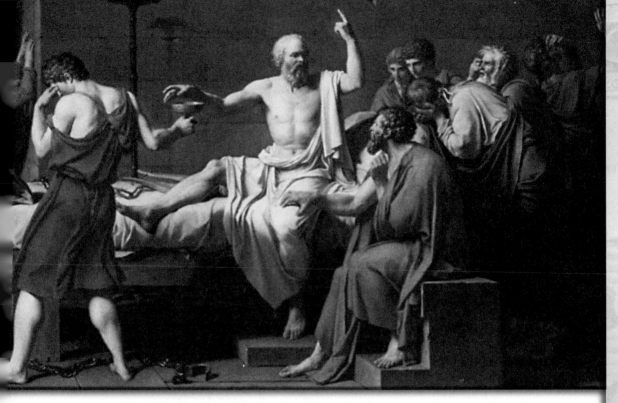

▲ *The philosopher Socrates was condemned to death by the Athenian government for corrupting young minds. French artist Jacques-Louis David painted* The Death of Socrates *in 1787. It shows Socrates about to drink the poison that will end his life.*

- **Citizens had to present their own cases** in court. However, they were permitted to hire lawyers and speech-writers to help them make their case.

- **Citizens were only allowed** a limited amount of time to present their case. Speeches were timed using a water clock.

- **Allegations of treason** were heard in front of the Assembly. Since the crime was against all citizens, it was thought fair that all citizens should act as the jury.

Lesser officials

- **Every Greek *polis*** employed officials who ensured the smooth running of the government – enforcing laws, gathering taxes and keeping records.

- **In smaller cities**, these officials were often unpaid, and worked part-time. In larger cities, the officials worked full-time and most were paid a salary.

- **The *gymnasiarchos*** was in charge of the maintenance of the state gymnasion – the institution for education and sport.

▶ *The* Hoplomachoi *(centre) was an official who trained the citizens to fight in wars.*

- **Another task** of the *gymnasiarchos* was to find exceptional athletes among those who attended the gymnasion, who could represent the *polis* at festivals and games. If such a person were found, he may then have been paid a wage so that he could train full-time.

- **The *hoplomachoi*** was a key official in most cities. His main role was to train the soldiers. He also inspected the town walls and gates to make sure that they were in good condition.

- **Another official** kept a detailed record of all citizens. This office became increasingly important as citizens' rights increased. By about 400 BC, the citizenship records were updated regularly and were available to the public.

- ***Taxiarchs* kept records on all citizens** containing details of whether men were fit and able to march with the army in the event of a war.

- **The *agorarchon*** was responsible for regulating the market, or *agora*. Part of his job was to ensure that the scales that were used by all the traders weighed goods accurately.

- **Most cities** levied taxes on goods that were imported or exported. A special official had the task of calculating the tax and making sure that it was paid.

- **Harbour masters** had to ensure the smooth running of the port. He decided which ship should dock where, supervised dock workers and collected fees from shipowners.

135

Contracts and bribes

- **Ancient Greek** states did not usually employ workmen directly. Contractors (architects who organized construction) were hired to work on large projects.

- **In 430 BC**, the rulers of Athens decided to build a new temple to their patron goddess Athene. They hired the architect Actinus, who designed the building and organized its construction.

▼ *The Parthenon, the greatest temple in Athens, was designed by a single architect who won the contract for the work.*

- **Actinus produced** a monumental temple of elegant proportions, famous today as the Parthenon. The cost of such contracts was enormous.

- **Bribery was common**. Builders were keen to gain valuable contracts, and many were willing to share the profits they would earn in order to secure them.

- **A close watch** was kept on government officials. They were not allowed to take bribes, and punishments could be severe.

- **An Athenian official** called Architeles was sent a box of food by a politician. His staff thought the gift was of such low value that it could not be a bribe, but a purse of gold coins was hidden under the food.

- **The Athenian admiral Themistocles** took a bribe from the government of Euobea to bring the Athenian fleet to help them during the Persian wars. He did not tell the Euobeans that this was what he had been ordered to do.

- **An accusation of corruption** was a favourite way to try to discredit a rival politician. Although such allegations were difficult to prove, they were often successful anyway because they created a climate of suspicion.

- **Themistocles was put in charge** of rebuilding the port of Piraeus in about 485 BC. The new port was much admired, but Themistocles was accused of taking bribes and was forced to leave Athens.

- **Priests were sometimes bribed** to spoil sacrifices to make it look as if the gods disapproved of certain people or actions. One priest from Delphi who took such a bribe was exiled for life.

The Spartan system

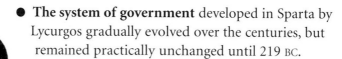

- **The system of government** developed in Sparta by Lycurgos gradually evolved over the centuries, but remained practically unchanged until 219 BC.

- **The main aim** of the Spartan system was to produce a nation of soldiers able to defeat all enemies and to keep Sparta safe from invasion. Spartan society and government was dedicated to war.

- **Most of the population** of Sparta were Helots. They worked as farmers and manual workers, producing the wealth and food needed by the state. They had no role in government and were heavily taxed. About 30 percent of the population were called Lacedaimonians, meaning people who lived outside the city of Sparta. The adult men were citizens of Sparta and could attend the Assembly, but could not be government officials.

◀ *A small statuette of a Spartan girl running in a race. The Spartans were unusual in allowing girls to compete.*

...FASCINATING FACT...

Sparta was famous for its frugal living conditions and strict regime. We now use the word 'spartan' to describe situations that are considered to be particularly stark or severe.

- **The Lacedaimonians** could work at any job they liked, and paid taxes on what they earned. During wartime, the Lacedaimonian men were called up to serve in the army.
- **The Spartiates** were the citizens of the city of Sparta. They made up about 10 percent of the population. The Spartiates did not work for a living, but were given housing, food and land by the state.
- **The Spartan army** relied upon the Spartiates, who dedicated their entire lives to warfare and training for war. They were the most feared warriors in all of Greece.
- **Spartiate boys** left their families at the age of five to go and live in an army barracks. Here they were taught to read and write, and spent several hours each day doing sports and physical exercises.
- **At the age of 12**, a boy became a youth. He would then be given hoplite weapons of a size suitable for his age, and his seven years of military training began.
- **A Spartiate** became a full-time soldier at the age of 19. He joined a mess of 16 men with whom he ate his meals, trained every day and fought beside in battle.

The rule of the diadochi

- **The *diadochi*** were the rulers who followed Alexander the Great and ruled during the Hellenistic Period. They were descended from Macedonian nobles.

▼ *Upon the death of Alexander the Great, his leading generals became governors of the various states of his vast empire.*

SUCCESSOR STATES

Empire of Alexander

Egypt
Seized by Ptolemy. Ruled by his descendants until the death of Queen Cleopatra VII in 30 BC when it was conquered by Rome.

Phrygia
Seized by Eumenes, conquered by Macedonia in 315 BC.

Macedonia
Seized by Antipater, then later by Antigonus, whose descendents ruled the kingdom until the death of King Perseus in 168 BC. Conquered by Rome.

Babylonia
Seized by Seleucus, and later known as the Seleucid Empire. Originally covered most of the Asian area of Alexander's conquests but later fragmented.

Epirus
Seized by Craterus, conquered by Macedonia in 321 BC.

Pergamum
Independent from about 260 BC. Annexed by Rome in 133 BC

Bactria
Independent from about 200 BC. Conquered by Parthians c. 100 BC

- **The system of government** in Macedonia had been one of absolute rule by the king, although the aristocrats had the right to advise the king and even to argue against some of his decisions.

- **Mainland Greece** fell to power of Antigonus, King of Macedon. Greek cities in Asia Minor and the Middle East fell under the power of other kings, but the Greek cities of southern Italy and Sicily remained free.

- **Some territories** were ruled by the kings directly through royal officials, but they knew that most *poleis* would object to such arrangements. They would prefer to rule themselves.

- **The kings usually decided** not to try to rule the cities directly, but to intervene only when they needed to do so.

- **Royal ambassadors** lived in most *poleis*. Officially, they simply farmed the king's land, but in reality they were expected to report back on what was going on and if anyone spoke out against the king.

- **The key demands** of the kings were that the cities should pay tribute, usually in gold or silver, to the king. Nor should the cities have their own armies with which they could defy the king.

- **If two cities** had a dispute, they would send ambassadors to the king who would listen to both sides and then issue a judgement. Sometimes the king would appoint a third, neutral city to hear the case.

- **Kings sometimes** sent royal judges to take over the administration of the law in a city. This ensured that civil order was maintained.

- **The source** of a king's power was his army. The Hellenistic kings could field enormous armies of up to 100,000 men. No city could stand against such might.

145

Crisis and decline

- **The system of** *polis* **government** continued under the rule of the Hellenistic kings. The various cities had different types of constitution, but they were all in charge of their own internal affairs.

- **Although the kings** rarely intervened directly in *polis* affairs, their enormous power and influence began to affect how the cities ran themselves. The *polis* system began to break down.

- **For instance,** the wealthy Athenian Philippides lived at the court of King Lysimchus of Macedon from 310 to 283 BC. As a friend of the king, Philippides managed to win favours for his city.

- **The official representatives** of Athens and other cities began to be sidelined by rich men such as Philippides. The formal government began to lose power and prestige.

- **As the power of the government** declined, the position of officials became more ceremonial and less influential.

- **Rich men** found that it was possible to bribe officials more easily. For example, they could pay the Council to put particular motions to the Assembly, and not to put forward other ideas.

> ...FASCINATING FACT...
> Some cities began to erect statues of their king in the temples. The city of Teos made King Antiochus III a god. Sacrifices of animals and crops were made in front of a statue of Antiochus.

▶ *A statue of Augustus Caesar, the first Roman emperor. He reformed the government of the Greek world along Roman lines.*

- **By about 200** BC, the Assembly in most cities had much less power than before. In some, the Assembly no longer met, and the Council took all the decisions.

- **As Rome became more powerful**, its generals and governors preferred to do business with a few trusted rich men, than with democratic assemblies that might take unexpected decisions.

- **The Romans** eventually abolished all the *poleis*. They carved Greece up into a number of provinces with Roman governors.

Greek architecture

- **In the Mycenaean Period**, the Greeks built strong defensive walls of stone around their cities, although most houses and other buildings were made of wood.

- **Until about 650** BC, the Greeks built all of their buildings out of wood or brick, using thatch for roofs. A few roughly shaped stones were used for foundations and around doorways.

- **When the Greeks** began to build in stone, they based their designs on the wooden structures that the new stone buildings were replacing. For example, their new temples had stone columns that were based on pillars carved from single tree trunks.

- **At first**, the Greeks only used stone for temples, but later it was used for many different types of public buildings.

- **There were three** basic styles, or orders, of Greek architecture. Some buildings were built using just one order, others combined two or even all three.

- **The Doric order** developed in mainland Greece around 650 BC. Doric columns had a plain square capital (top), and did not have bases. The space above the columns had small sculptures.

> ...FASCINATING FACT...
> Most stone buildings were square because it made them easier to build.
> However, a few temples, called *tholos*, were round.

| Doric | Ionic | Corinthian |

▲ *The three orders of Greek architecture originally came from different areas but, by around 700 BC, they were being widely used across Greece.*

- **The Ionic order** appeared in Ionia around 600 BC. The columns stood on square bases and had capitals in the shape of rounded scrolls. The space above the columns had a toothed decoration.

- **The Corinthian order** developed later. Columns, topped by capitals carved into the shape of acanthus leaves, stood on large bases. The space above the columns had a long, continuous sculpture.

- **A column** carved into the shape of a woman was known as a *caryatid*. This was most usual in buildings of the Doric order.

149

Building methods

- **Most Greek stone buildings** were constructed using stone from local quarries, but some were faced with more expensive stone such as marble, which was more durable and looked better.

- **Stones were cut** to roughly the right size and shape at the quarry. They were then moved by boat or cart to the building site.

- **Once at the building site**, each stone was carefully carved, using bronze or iron tools, to precisely the correct shape before being lifted into place.

- **Small holes** were made in the top of stone blocks in which metal hooks could be fitted. The hooks were linked to ropes that ran through pulleys. Teams of slaves hauled on the ropes to lift the stones.

- **The stone blocks** were held in place by bronze hooks and strips known as cramps. These could be hidden inside the stone so that they would not be visible once the building was finished.

- **Columns were built up** out of a number of circular sections called drums. Each drum had a hole at its centre through which a wooden pole was pushed. Each drum was put into position by being lowered over the top of the pole.

- **Columns were often built** with a slight bulge at the middle. When seen from a distance, a straight column can look thinner at the middle, so making it slightly thicker at this point actually made it look straight.

- **The statues and sculptures** that adorned Greek buildings were carved in a workshop on the building site. Once finished, they were lifted into position.

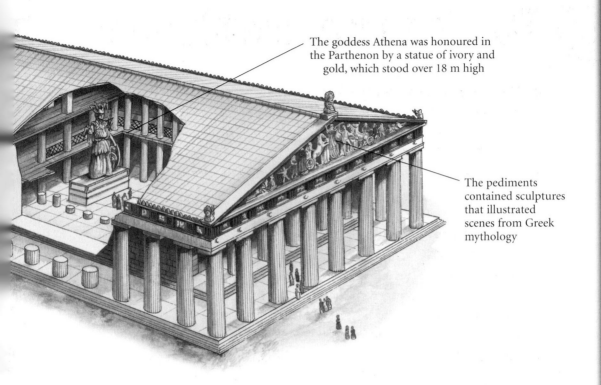

The goddess Athena was honoured in the Parthenon by a statue of ivory and gold, which stood over 18 m high

The pediments contained sculptures that illustrated scenes from Greek mythology

▲ *The main material used to build the Parthenon was stone. Wood was used for the roof and some flooring.*

- **Once the main building** work was completed, painters went to work. Most of the sculptures and other decorative features were painted in bright shades of red and blue and may even have been gilded.

- **Architects preferred** not to disclose their building methods. When asked how he had erected the gigantic gate of the Temple of Artemis, the architect Chersiphron replied, "Artemis did it."

Monuments and wonders

- **The ancient Greeks** compiled a list of the Seven Wonders of the World. These were the most impressive buildings in existence. Five of the seven were Greek.

- **The Great Pyramid** was the oldest wonder. It was built at Giza in Egypt, in about 2700 BC, to house the tomb of the pharaoh, Khufu. It stood 147 m tall and was built with more than two million blocks of stone.

- **The Hanging Gardens of Babylon** were built around 540 BC for one of the wives of Nebuchadnezzar II, king of Babylon. They consisted of gardens planted on the balconies of a building that overlooked the city.

▼ *The great Temple of Artemis at Ephesus as it would have looked when new. This was one of the largest and most decorated buildings in the world.*

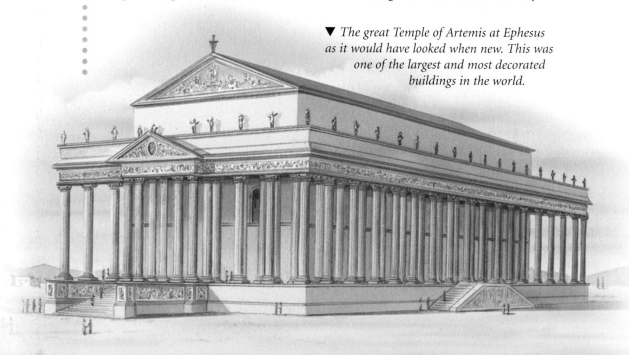

- **The Statue of Zeus** at Olympia was created in 438 BC by Phidias. The statue stood 13 m tall and was made of ivory and gold, resting on a wooden internal frame.

- **The Temple of Artemis** at Ephesus was built around 550 BC. It was made entirely of marble and measured 131 m long by 79 m wide. Each of the 127 columns stood 20 m tall and were decorated with carvings and paintwork.

- **The Mausoleum of Halicarnassus** was built around 353 BC, and was the tomb of King Maussollos. It was a building 45 m in height, and decorated with statues carved by the most famous sculptors in the world.

- **The Colossus of Rhodes** was a bronze statue of the sun god Helios that was built by the architect Chares in 282 BC. It stood 33 m tall beside the entrance to the harbour of Rhodes.

- **The Pharos at Alexandria** was a lighthouse that guided ships into the Egyptian port. It was built in about 297 BC by the Greek architect Sostratus, and stood about 100 m tall.

- **Only ruins** of the Seven Wonders remain. Some statues from the Mausoleum have been found, as have the foundations of the Pharos and the Temple of Artemis. The Great Pyramid is almost intact. All the rest have vanished completely.

...FASCINATING FACT...
A man named Herostratus burned down the Temple of Artemis at Ephesus in 356 BC, because he wanted to be famous at any cost.

Early sculptures

- **Mycenaean Greeks** produced very few sculptures. The entrance gate to Mycenae itself is topped by two carved lions, but otherwise the earliest Greeks preferred abstract designs.

- **In about 650** BC, Greeks working in Egypt began to produce stone statues of people. The idea spread quickly and by 600 BC, stone statues were being produced in most Greek cities.

- **The most common type of statue** was the *kouros*, a naked man usually shown walking, with stiff arms and legs. The head always faced directly forward, as in Egyptian statues.

- **Less numerous was the *kore***, a female statue. These figures were shown wearing long dresses and were usually placed in temples.

- ***Kouros* figures** were used in temples and on graves to represent gods and men. They were idealized figures, and were not intended to be viewed as realistic portraits.

- **The *kouros* and *kore*** belong to the style of sculpture called the archaic. They were designed to be viewed from the front and often stood in niches or alcoves in walls.

- **In around 520 BC**, the rigid *kouros* began to change. Sculptors began to sculpt figures in different poses – resting on one foot, or glancing to one side.

- **Around the same time**, sculptors began to produce sculptures and reliefs to fit into the triangular spaces on the gable ends (pediments) of temples. In order to fit into the space available, they showed men, animals and monsters in various poses.

- **By around 500 BC**, sculptors began working in bronze. These statues stood in similar poses to contemporary stone statues. Few bronze statues have survived as most were later melted down.

▶ *The face of an early Greek statue, known as a* kouros. *These statues were formal in design.*

Phidias and his followers

- **The ancient Greeks** believed that Phidias of Athens was the best sculptor in the world. He produced the sculptures that adorned the Parthenon on the Athenian Acropolis.

- **Phidias was banished from Athens** for political reasons in 432 BC. In revenge, he went to Olympia and offered to make a great statue of Zeus that would be even grander than the work he had done in Athens.

- **The statue of Zeus** at Olympia was Phidias' greatest work. It survived until AD 475, by which time it had been moved to Constantinople. It was destroyed in an accidental fire.

◀ *A statue from Hellenistic times showing the Trojan priest Laocoon and his two sons, all of whom were killed by snakes.*

- **It is thought** that Phidias had a team of junior sculptors who followed his designs and did most of the more basic work.

- **The sculpture** of Hermes and Dionysus, found by archaeologists at Olympia, is almost certainly the original work by Praxiteles.

- **Phidias later moved** to Lemnos, where he produced dozens of bronze and stone sculptures. He died in about 415 BC.

- **Praxiteles lived** around the year 350 BC. He specialized in nude figures, and his Aphrodite of Cnidus was considered to be the finest statue of a naked woman, in the world.

- **Lysippus of Sicyon** produced more than 600 statues throughout his career. Alexander the Great commissioned him to produce the only official statues of himself.

- **Lysippus was famous** for his unusual compositions. His best-known work showed a man getting out of a bath, but he also produced conventional statues of gods and men.

The tragedies

- **The tragedy** is a grand drama doomed to end unhappily for the hero. The form was created by Greek dramatists such as Aeschylus, Euripides and Sophocles.

- **The earliest Greek plays** were performances of sacred songs and dances that were held in honour of the god Dionysius every spring. These were staged in the *agora* and were performed by a chorus of 15 men.

▼ *The Temple of Herodes Atticus in Athens was built about AD 160, with banks of seats and a tall stage set.*

- **Around the year 540** BC, Peisistratus, tyrant of Athens, introduced a drama competition. Each year, three writers were asked to put on plays during the spring festival to Dionysus. The man who wrote the best play was given a prize.

- **The first performance** by an actor as a character in a play was around 510 BC. His role on stage was to ask questions, which the chorus would answer. Dramatists used the actor to set the scene and create emotions.

- **By about 500** BC, plays were being staged in purpose-built theatres. These were made by building seats into the side of a hill and erecting a stage in front of the seats.

- **From about 483** BC, the writer Aeschylus wrote a series of plays that won the drama competition for several years running. He used up to three actors on stage, in addition to the chorus. Seven of his plays have survived and are the oldest known dramas.

- **When Aeschylus staged** three connected plays, called the *Oresteia*, in 458 BC, he introduced masks and costumes. The play told the mythical story of the revenge of Orestes and was so powerful that people in the audience fainted.

- **Sophocles first** won a drama competition in 468 BC. He introduced the idea of irony – when a character does not realize the significance of what he says, but the audience does.

- **Aristotle and other Greeks** believed that the play *King Oedipus* by Sophocles was the greatest tragedy ever written.

- **Euripedes wrote** 92 plays between 441 and 406 BC. His work was very popular and his plays continued to be staged long after his death.

The comedies

- **The satyr plays** began to be staged by about 490 BC. These were rude comedies that featured forest spirits called satyrs, and they were intended to provide light relief between tragedies.

- **Some satyr plays** poked fun at real people, such as politicians and rich noblemen, although care had to be taken to not offend anyone important. Aeschylus was prosecuted for sacrilege for the content of one of his plays.

- **Comedy plays** first appeared in 488 BC, when a prize was given at the spring festival to Dionysus for the best comedy. At first, comedies took the same form as tragedies, with two actors and a chorus.

- **The earliest comic playwright** to become famous was the Athenian Cratinus, who specialized in puns. He wrote a serious of crude plays about men who drank too much and chased women.

- **A new comic writer** put on his first successful play in 424 BC. This was Aristophanes, who specialized in making up words by combining two existing words and using it as part of a joke.

- **Aristophanes also gained fame** by dressing his chorus in elaborate costumes to resemble animals or objects.

- **Around the year 410** BC, a young poet named Plato began writing comedies. He became very famous, but none of his work has survived.

> ...FASCINATING FACT...
> The only complete play by Menander was found written on some sheets of papyrus in an Egyptian tomb in 1958.

160

▶ *A typical theatre, such as the theatre of Dionysus in Athens, seated 14,000 people. Greek actors wore masks with exaggerated painted features so that the audience could clearly see what sort of character they were playing.*

- **In around 320 BC**, the writer Menander developed a new type of comedy. Menander's plays focused on ordinary people's reactions to events that could take place in real life.

- **Many of Menander's** plays were love stories. Misunderstandings and mistakes lead to all sorts of comic circumstances that almost always end happily for all characters concerned.

The early philosophers

- **The sophists** were men who, from around 700 BC, would move around the cities of Greece holding lessons on morality, truth and other subjects. The word 'sophist' means wise man.

- **One of the most famous sophists** was Protagoras, who died in about 415 BC. He taught that 'man is the measure of all things', and believed that it was humans, not gods, who should decide what was good or bad.

- **Pythagoras of Samos** was a mathematician and sophist. He believed that all animals, including humans, were essentially the same. He thought that souls were reborn after death in a new human or animal.

- **In about 530 BC**, Pythagoras and his followers moved to southern Italy. At Croton, he set up a small community of men and women who devoted themselves to learning.

- **Empedocles lived in Sicily**, and died in about 433 BC. He believed that everything on Earth is composed of four elements – earth, air, fire and water. This idea remained influential for over 2000 years.

- **Socrates was the son** of an Athenian stonemason, and fought in the army when he was young. Around the age of about 35, he gave up work and devoted himself to ideas and morality.

> ...FASCINATING FACT...
> Socrates married a woman named Xanthippe, then spent the rest of his life complaining about her bad temper.

▲ *A painting from the Italian Renaissance of the school of Athens.*
The philosophers of Athens are shown debating the eternal truths of existence.

- **Socrates said "virtue is knowledge"**, by which he meant that before people can be good they must first understand what 'good' means.

- **Socrates often used his knowledge** to show how little wealthy or important people knew. He would ask them a questions designed to show that their assumptions and behaviour were based on false knowledge.

- **In 399 BC**, the rulers of Athens put Socrates on trial for sacrilege and condemned him to death. Socrates was forced committed suicide.

The Academy

- **Plato was a pupil** of Socrates. He expressed ideas by writing dramas based around philosophical conversations. Much of what we know about Socrates comes from the work of Plato.

- **In *The Republic***, a series of ten books, Plato proposed a system of government. He said there should be a class system and that the ruler should be a philosopher-king, wise enough to rule in the interests of all.

- **The education** that the philosopher-king should receive was described as being based on physical exercise, artistic appreciation and philosophy.

▶ *Plato was one of the greatest of all Greek philosophers and founder of the Academy. His works have remained influential into the 21st century.*

- **After travelling** to many Greek cities, Plato produced a new book called *Laws*. In this, he abandoned the idea of a philosopher-king and said there should be joint ownership of all property by the citizens.

- **When he returned** to Athens, Plato bought a field called Academus that lay just outside Athens. He set up a school in the field, called the Academy, where he taught his ideas.

- **Plato died in 347** BC, but his Academy survived until AD 529. Thousands of men were educated there and Plato's ideas have remained important up to the present day.

- **Aristotle was a pupil of Plato** at the Academy. He was hired as the tutor to the young Alexander the Great and travelled widely around the Mediterranean.

- **Aristotle believed** that the education at the Academy was too narrow, so he set up a rival school called the Lyceum. Lessons at the Lyceum included all types of science and mathematics as well as philosophy and the arts.

- **The teachings of Zeno** of Citium became known as stoicism because he would often sit in a porch – 'stoa' in Greek – to teach. Stoics believed that the world is ruled by divine reason, and that humans should accept this and be indifferent to success or hardship.

- **Epicurus of Samos** came to Athens in about 300 BC. He caused scandal by allowing women and slaves to attend his lessons. Epicurus taught that people should seek happiness by renouncing greed and desire.

Archimedes and mathematics

- **Pythagoras of Samos** was a philosopher and mathematician. He was fascinated by numbers and believed they could be applied to many different aspects of life. Around 530 BC he worked out the precise lengths of strings on a lyre needed to produce accurate musical notes.

- **Pythagoras** measured the movements of the planets. He found that they were closely related to the measurements of the lyre strings, so he developed a theory of divine tunes that he called the music of the spheres.

- **The best-known work** of Pythagoras is his theorem concerning the relationships between the measurements along different sides of triangles.

- **In about 300 BC**, King Ptolemy of Egypt hired a man named Euclid to teach mathematics to the court. Euclid insisted that he would not teach anything until he had proved that it was true.

- **Euclid wrote 15 books** about geometry. In them he developed a systematic method of proving mathematical propositions.

- **Archimedes of Syracuse** was generally recognized to be the greatest mathematician of ancient Greece. He was able to apply mathematical theory to solve practical problems.

> ...FASCINATING FACT...
> One of the many earlier theories that Euclid was able to prove
> was that of Pythagoras. As a result, some people prefer to give the
> credit for the discovery to Euclid.

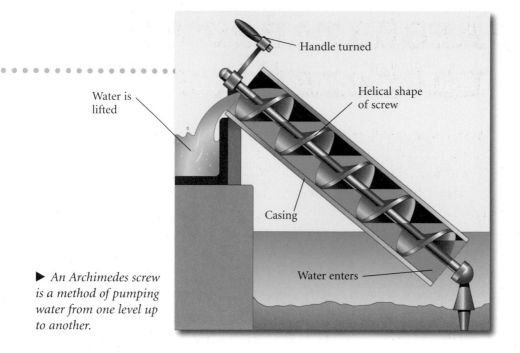

Handle turned

Water is lifted

Helical shape of screw

Casing

Water enters

▶ *An Archimedes screw is a method of pumping water from one level up to another.*

- **King Heiron of Syracuse** asked Archimedes to work out if a jeweller had used pure gold to make a crown. This meant calculating the density of the metal, and Archimedes needed to know the volume of the crown to do this.

- **When getting into his bath**, Archimedes noticed that some of the water was displaced by his body and flowed over the edge of the tub. He realized that if the crown was pure gold it would displace the same volume of water as an equal weight of pure gold. By putting the crown in water and measuring the volume of water, he could solve the problem.

- **Archimedes was so excited** that he leapt out of his bath and ran to King Heiron shouting "Eureka", meaning 'I have got it'. Not until he met the king, did Archimedes realize he was not wearing any clothes.

Measuring the Earth

- **Around 275 BC**, the mathematician Aristarchus of Samos suggested that the Earth spun on its axis and revolved around the Sun, as did all the other planets. Few people believed him and his ideas were ridiculed.

- **The size of the Earth** was first calculated by Eratosthenes of Cyrene, in about 225 BC. Eratoshenes was told of a well in the south of Egypt on which the Sun shone without casting any shadows in mid summer.

- **Eratosthenes realized** this meant that the Sun was directly overhead at the well, and he knew that it was not overhead on the same day in Alexandria. He measured the angle of the Sun at Alexandria, and the distance from Alexandria to the well.

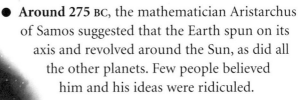

◀ *Hipparchus spent long hours studying the stars, and named every star that he could see.*

- **By using Euclid's** geometric theories, Eratosthenes then worked out the size of the Earth with such precision that he was only about 200 km out.

- **Apollonius of Perge** lived in about 200 BC. He dedicated years to the study of cones and wrote seven books describing how to calculate the volumes and other dimensions of cones.

- **Apollonius also studied** the movements of the planets. He worked out that the apparent irregularities in the movements as seen from Earth could be explained if each planet orbited a spot close to its position.

- **The system developed** by Apollonius to explain planetary movements became known as the epicycle theory. It remained the most popular way to explain and predict planetary movements for 1800 years.

- **Hipparchus of Nicaea** was born around 170 BC. He realized that some of the apparent changes in the position of the planets was due to the fact that the Earth rotated, a phenomenon called parallax.

- **When studying** the movements of the Moon, Hipparchus realized how these affected eclipses of the Sun. He produced tables that predicted eclipses of both the Sun and the Moon for the next 600 years.

...FASCINATING FACT...
Eratosthenes of Cyrene was nicknamed 'Beta', meaning second,
because he came second in every mathematical contest he entered,
but never came first.

The invention of history

- **During the Mycenaean Period**, it is thought that each king employed a man whose task was to compose poems about the great deeds of the king and his ancestors.

- **Some of the events** of the Mycenaean Period were still known during the Dark Age. The poet Homer used these to produce his great epic poems about the Trojan War, the *Illiad* and the *Odyssey*.

- **Around 570 BC**, Anaximander of Miletus wrote a book called *On Nature*, which was a description of the various countries of the world, but which also included sections on their recent past.

- **Hecataeus of Miletus** wrote a book called *Genealogies* in about 500 BC, in which he attempted to trace the history of Greece back to the Mycenaean Period. However, most of his material came from legends and folklore and not from official records.

- **In about 460 BC**, Herodotus of Halicarnassus decided to record a history of the wars that took place between the Greek cities and Persia. The men who fought as soldiers in the wars were growing old and Herodotus thought the story of the war should be preserved for future generations and not forgotten.

- **The *Histories* of Herodotus** was the first book in which the writer not only records what happened, but also tries to explain why it happened. Herodotus has been called 'the father of History'.

- **In the years** after Herodotus produced his work, many histories of many other *polis* were recorded. Few of these have survived, and some recorded as much legend as fact.

● **In about 404** BC, Thucydides of Athens wrote a history of the Peloponnesian War. He produced a coherent account that included analysis of the events and their causes as well as the speeches of famous men.

● **Thucydides' style of writing** was much admired. For the 1000 years, it was used by historians as a model.

● **During the time** of the Hellenistic Kingdoms, historians were hired by kings and nobles to write about events as they happened. As a result, many of these were complimentary to the kings who paid for them.

▲ *The great warrior Achilles as depicted in the 2004 movie* Troy *(Warner Bros. Pictures). Achilles was a legendary hero who may have been based on a real person.*

Doctors and healing

- **According to the poet Homer**, the first Greek doctor was Asclepius who lived in the Mycenaean Period. Asclepius taught that sick people should rest in a temple of Apollo and pray for a cure.

- **Later Greeks** believed that Asclepius was the son of Apollo, and a god. If they recovered from a serious disease they would sacrifice a cockerel to him.

- **Around 450 BC**, Hippocrates of Cos began working as a doctor at the shrine of Asclepius. He advocated that doctors should keep records of the symptoms suffered by patients so that they could recognize different types of disease.

◄ A doctor cares for a patient, as seen in an ancient carving. The Greeks were the first people to keep records of diseases and how to cure them.

172

- **Over the next 150 years**, the doctors that followed Hippocrates at Cos kept detailed records of the diseases they recognized and what they did to try to cure them.

- **The books** produced at Cos include instructions for carrying out surgery, and recipes for producing medicines using herbs and plants. Thousands of doctors were trained at Cos.

- **Herophilus of Chalcedon** was interested in the effects of drugs on the body. From about 270 BC, he tried giving herbs and plant extracts to people and then studied what happened.

- **Herophilus was the first doctor** to take a patient's pulse to study how his heart was working.

- **In 260 BC**, Eristratos of Ceos began to cut up the dead bodies of condemned criminals to examine internal organs.

- **Eristratos identified many organs** in the body and their jobs. He thought that the body was like a complex machine and that sickness happened when the machine broke down.

Inventions and devices

- **Philon of Byzantium** hated his guests eating with dirty hands, so around 400 BC he invented a device that poured cool water from a jar when a lever was lifted, to encourage people to wash.

- **Three hundred years later**, Heron of Alexandria copied Philon's idea. He produced a jar that poured out a measured quantity of holy water every time a visitor to a temple put a bronze coin in a slot.

- **Heron realized** that hot air rose through cool air, so he made a device that used the smoke rising from a small fire to make statues appear to dance.

- **Heron also knew** that hot air expanded, and invented a device for opening temple doors as if by the unseen hands of the gods.

- **When a fire was lit** on an altar, air within a metal sphere inside the altar was heated. As the air expanded, the water was pushed out of the sphere and along a siphon. It flowed into a bucket that was attached to the doors by ropes. As the bucket filled, the ropes pulled down, opening the doors.

- **A steam engine** was developed by Heron. A sealed metal basin was filled with water and placed on a fire. Two pipes from the basin were connected to a hollow, metal ball that could spin, and that had two narrow, bent metal pipes sticking out from it at opposite points.

> ...FASCINATING FACT...
> The various devices invented by Heron and others were considered to be toys or tricks. They could not be made into useful machines because the metals of the time were not fine enough for hi-tech engineering.

◄ The steam engine designed by Heron caused a metal ball to spin at great speed, but it was not considered to be a useful device.

● **As the water boiled**, steam rose through the pipes to the ball. As the steam escaped from the pipes, it drove the ball around. A modern replica could spin at an astonishing 1500 revolutions per minute.

● **Heron used pulleys** and weights to produce other gadgets. He developed a statue on wheels that could automatically move around a temple.

● **A fully automatic theatre** devised by Heron staged a play performed by puppets when a handle was turned.

The origin of the gods

- **The Mycenaean Greeks** are thought to have worshipped a goddess named Rhea, who was usually portrayed in the form of a woman, naked from the waist up.

- **Little is known** about any other Mycenaean deities, but they were probably local gods and goddesses who were thought to have power over certain places or types of activity.

- **The later Greeks** developed a complex story to explain the origins of their gods and goddesses. They believed that before anything else existed, there was only Chaos. Then came the Earth – a goddess named Gaea, and the night sky – a god named Uranus.

- **The first children of Gaea and Uranus** were the Titans. There were 12 Titans, six male and six female, of whom Kronos was the youngest.

- **Gaea and Uranus** later had other children. These included a race of monsters that had 100 arms each, and the Cyclopes, who all had a single eye in the middle of their foreheads.

- **Kronos then attacked his father**, Uranus, with a steel sickle given to him by his mother, Gaea. In doing so, Kronos became the ruler of the universe.

- **Kronos then married another Titan**, Rhea. They had six children: the goddesses Hestia, Demeter and Hera, and the gods Hades, Poseidon and Zeus.

- **Kronos feared** he would be ousted by his own child as he had ousted his father, so he swallowed each of his children as they were born. However, when Zeus was born, Rhea tricked Kronos by giving him a stone wrapped in cloth to swallow, and hid her son.

- **When Zeus was older**, he fought and defeated Kronos. Zeus forced his father to drink a potion that made him vomit up Zeus' five brothers and sisters. Zeus became the ruler of the universe.

- **The other Titans began** a war against Zeus and the new gods. The Titans were defeated, tied up in chains and sent to live far beneath the Earth.

◀ *The god Kronos was tricked into eating a rock wrapped in cloth, instead of the baby Zeus. Kronos was later ousted by Zeus, who took his place as king of the gods.*

The origins of the world

- **The Greeks believed** that the world took on its present shape during the rule of Kronos.

- **It was during this time** that the Titans married each other and produced a host of divine children.

  - **Ocean and Tethys** gave birth to 3000 sons – the rivers, and 3000 daughters – the water nymphs who cared for the rivers.

  - **Hyperion and Theia** gave birth to Helios the Sun, Selene the Moon and Eos the dawn.

  - **The Titan** that personified night gave birth to death, sleep and dreams. She then gave birth to happiness and misery as well as old age, hunger, disease, lies, injustices and false oaths.

  - **Night also gave birth** to the three Fates – Clotho, Lachesis and Atropos. Whenever a human was born, the Fates gave them a portion of good and evil that stayed with that person for life.

  - **The Titans** Iapetus and Themis had four sons, one of which was Prometheus. One day, Prometheus mixed some of his tears with pieces of clay to make the first men.

◀ *The wise Titan Prometheus helped the human race by teaching mortals special skills.*

▶ *A modern reconstruction of the interior of the Temple of Zeus at Olympia. The statue of Zeus was made of ivory and gold, and was held to be one of the most beautiful works of art in all of Greece.*

- **Zeus fought** with his brothers and sisters against the Titans for ten years. The Titans were overthrown when the gods and goddesses secured the help of the hundred-handed giants and the Cyclopes.

- **Prometheus did not join the war** of the gods against the Titans, but he always held a grudge against Zeus for the harsh way the Titans were treated. Prometheus stole fire from the forge of Hephaistos and gave it to men.

- **Zeus was furious**, and chained Prometheus to a rock for all eternity. He sent the first woman, Pandora, to the men, who took with her a vase containing diseases, dismay, fear and all other bad things.

181

The Olympian gods

- **By about 500 BC**, most Greeks believed that there were 12 gods and goddesses that were more important than all the others. They thought these deities lived in magnificent palaces on Mount Olympos, so they were known as the Olympians.

- **Zeus was the king of the gods**. He could hurl thunderbolts to Earth and control the weather. He sometimes fell in love with human women and the children he had with them became heroes.

- **Hera was the queen of the gods**, and Zeus' wife and sister. She was the goddess of marriage and motherhood, and the protector of women. She often quarrelled with Zeus.

- **Athene was the goddess of wisdom**, and of craftsmen. She was the patron goddess of Athens, which was named after her, and she protected Athenian soldiers in battle.

◀ *A bronze statue of Zeus. The eyes would originally have been filled with semi-precious stones.*

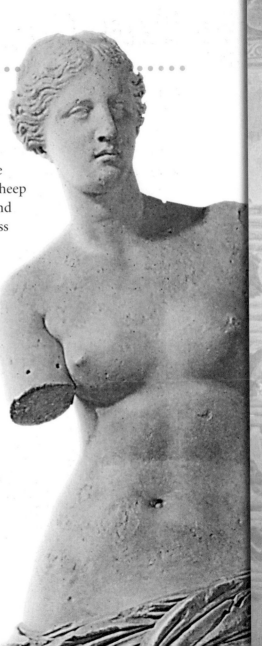

▶ *A statue of Aphrodite, the goddess of love and desire, carved in marble.*

- **Apollo was the god of the sun**, music and the arts. He was also linked to livestock, such as sheep and cattle. Artemis was Apollo's twin sister, and goddess of the moon. She was also the goddess of wilderness and the patron of hunters.

- **Aphrodite was the goddess of love**. She was in love with Ares, god of war. He loved bloodshed, courage and bravery, and was said to have a ferocious temper.

- **Hephaistos the Lame** made the weapons of war, and was the god of smiths.

- **Poseidon was god of the sea** and also of earthquakes. He was worshipped by sailors who greatly feared his anger.

- **Hermes was the messenger** of the gods, and patron of travellers. He was also the god of merchants. Hestia was the goddess of the hearth and of home life.

- **Demeter was the goddess of farming**, and of all plants that could be eaten.

Lesser mythical figures

- **The Olympian gods** were the most important and powerful of the Greek gods, but there were also many others.

- **Themis was a female Titan** who had helped Rhea hide Zeus from Kronos. She was the goddess of justice, and acted as the judge in disputes between the various gods.

- **Iris served the Olympian deities**, especially Zeus and Hera. She brought messages from the gods down to Earth by sliding down the rainbow.

- **Hebe was the goddess of youth**. Together with her handsome young brother Ganymede, she carried out the tasks on Olympos that were the job of unmarried girls in Greek families.

- **Boreas was the god of the north wind**, and loved creating storms. Zephyros was the god of the gentle west wind, while Notus was god of the south wind and Eurus was god of the east wind.

- **The Harpies** were evil creatures. They had the faces of old women and the bodies of birds. They destroyed crops with disease and brought famine to the Earth.

- **The Tritons and Nereids** were the servants of Poseidon. They were believed to be friendly to sailors and fishermen.

> ... FASCINATING FACT ...
> The Greeks thought that there was one thing more powerful than all the gods put together – destiny. Even Zeus did not argue with destiny.

- **Nymphs were female spirits** who guarded rivers, springs and other sources of fresh water. They were believed to be very beautiful, and every water source had an attendant nymph.

- **Eunomia, Dike and Irene** were the three Horae. They controlled rainfall on Earth and controlled the growth of plants.

▶ *Sea sirens were beautiful women who sang songs to lure sailors to sail closer to the rocks, causing their boats to crash.*

Deities of the world

- **The goddesses Gaea and Rhea** were probably worshipped by the Mycenaean Greeks, but by about 900 BC, they were no longer to be powerful deities.

- **Demeter was the goddess of grain** and the harvest. She was worshipped most on Crete, and in the Peloponnese and Attica. Her temples were always surrounded by trees.

- **Kore was the daughter** of Demeter. She was the goddess of corn, and was worshipped on Sicily, the main grain-producing region of the Greek world, and in Attica.

- **Dionysus was first worshipped** in Thrace, and became popular in Boeotia before spreading to the rest of Greece. He was the god of wine.

- **As the son of Zeus** but with a human mother, Dionysus was only a demi-god. He wandered across the world to see its marvels. Later, he was made into a true god by his father.

- **The Satyrs** were a semi-divine race of woodland spirits. They looked like hairy men with pointed ears and the hindquarters of a goat. They loved to play tricks on humans who wandered into the forests.

- **Pan was a god of the Peloponnese**, who was particularly revered by the shepherds of Arcadia. He was a piper, and was often depicted in a similar way to the satyrs, with the horns, ears and legs of a goat.

- **Aristaeus** was a god from Thessaly. In his home territory, he was thought to protect all domestic animals, but elsewhere in Greece he was most associated with bee-keeping.

186

◀ *Atlas was one of the Titans. He was given the task of holding up the sky to stop it falling on Earth. The sky is symbolized here by a globe.*

- **Ate was a daughter of Zeus** who was thrown out of Mount Olympos for causing too many arguments between the gods. Instead, she wandered the world encouraging men to take irresponsible decisions, and causing conflicts.

- **Zeus regretted his decision** to inflict Ate on the world, so he sent another daughter, named Lita, to track her down. Lita was the goddess of compromise and fair dealing, but she never managed to catch up with Ate.

187

Heroes and legends

- **To the ancient Greeks**, heroes were not just brave or wise men, they were believed to be partly divine. Most Greek states had an ancestral hero.

- **Theseus was the principle hero** of Athens. He was said to have been the son of King Aegeus of Athens, in about 1230 BC. Many legends tell of his stupendous strength.

- **The greatest exploit** of Theseus was to slay the Minotaur, a terrible half-man, half-bull monster that lived on Crete.

- **Corinth had two great heroes**. The first, Sisyphus, was said to have founded the city in around 1300 BC.

- **Sisyphus cheated death**. When he died, he tricked Hades, god of the underworld, into letting him return to Earth.

- **The second hero of Corinth** was Bellerophon, grandson of Sisyphus. Legends tell that with the aid of his flying horse, Pegasus, Bellerophon killed the terrifying monster, the Chimaera.

- **Perseus was the hero of Argos**, and son of Danae and Zeus. He was believed to have killed the Gorgon. It was said that looking at the face of a Gorgon could turn the viewer to stone.

- **Perseus avoided** looking at the Gorgon by using the reflection from the polished inside of his shield to see where he was striking.

- **Jason was a hero from Thessaly**. He was deprived of the throne of Iolkos by his uncle, King Pelias, who had secretly murdered Jason's father.

- **King Pelias sent Jason** to retrieve the golden fleece (the coat of a winged ram), believing he would not return. Departing in his ship, the *Argo*, Jason managed to obtain the fleece and took it back to Thessaly in triumph.

▲ *Theseus confronts the monstrous Minotaur in the labyrinth of the palace of King Minos of Crete.*

Heracles the hero

- **The greatest hero** of ancient Greece was Heracles, also known as Hercules. He was born in Thebes and lived in Tiryns. He was descended from the royal family of Argos.

- **Heracles was the son of Zeus** and was endowed with enormous strength and boundless energy. When he was a baby, he strangled two snakes that climbed into his cot.

- **Later**, Heracles killed his wife and children in a fit of madness sent by the goddess Hera. To compensate for the crime, he had to undertake 12 Labours set by King Eurystheus of Argos.

◀ *A statue showing Heracles killing the centaur, Nessus, who tried to abduct Heracles' wife, Deianira.*

- **The first Labour** was to kill the Nemean Lion, which had an impenetrable hide. Heracles strangled it with his bare hands. The second Labour was to kill the Hydra, a monster with nine heads, and he clubbed it to death.

- **The third Labour** was to capture the wild boar of Erymanthus, which was larger and stronger than any normal boar. Heracles wrapped it in thick ropes. The fourth Labour was to catch the wild deer of Ceryneia, which Heracles outran.

- **The fifth Labour** was to kill the man-eating Stymphalian birds, which Heracles killed with arrows. The sixth Labour was to clean the Stables of Augeias, which contained 100 cattle and had never been swept. Heracles diverted two rivers to flow through the stables.

- **The seventh Labour** was to ride the wild bull of Crete. The eighth Labour was to harness the mean-eating mares of Diomedes. Heracles first killed their grooms and fed them to the mares, then harnessed them.

- **The ninth Labour** was to steal the girdle of Hippolyte, Queen of the Amazons, which he took after killing her. The tenth Labour was to capture the Cattle of Geryon, which lived in what is now Spain.

- **The eleventh Labour** was to harvest the Golden Apples of the Hesperides, which grew at the western end of the world. The twelfth and greatest Labour was to go to the underworld and wrestle Cerberus, the three-headed dog that guarded the entrance to Hades.

...FASCINATING FACT...
After numerous adventures, Heracles died and was taken up to Mount Olympos to live forever among the gods.

Sacrifices and rituals

- **Religion in ancient Greece** was organized by the priests who served in the temples of the gods. These priests were usually part-time officials who were appointed by a ruler or elected by citizens.

- **Each temple had** a small staff of full-time workers, such as cleaners and craftsmen, but they played no part in the rituals.

▼ *The ruins of a Greek temple built in the Doric style. Public acts of worship took place outside the temple, the interior of which was for private worship and ritual.*

- **The temple** was thought to be a home for the honoured god. There was usually a statue of the god inside the temple.

- **The most frequent religious activity** was sacrifice. This often involved pouring small amounts of wine or olive oil onto the altar, and was also accompanied by prayers.

- **Some sacrifices** were state affairs. Cattle were sometimes brought to the temple, where their throats were slit to let the blood flow over the altar.

- **The cattle** were then butchered. The thigh bones and fat were burned on the altar as an offering to the god. The meat was cooked and eaten outside the temple.

- **People believed** that their gods demanded that rituals be carried out according to set procedures, and that certain sacrifices had to be made in special ways on particular days of the year.

- **Greeks did not feel** they had to lead good lives in order to please their gods, but they felt it was important not to offend their gods by breaking an oath, insulting a parent or making a sacrifice incorrectly.

- **People believed** that if gods felt insulted they would take revenge in some way, such as bestowing bad luck.

...FASCINATING FACT...
People were free to wander in and out of the temples to pray whenever they wished, but religious rituals took place in front of the temple in an open square.

The mysteries of Eleusis

- **Eleusis was a city in Attica**, just west of Athens. Once every five years, this small city became the site of the Eleusianian Mysteries, one of the greatest religious festivals of Greece.

- **According to legend**, Kore, daughter of Demeter, was a beautiful young woman. One day when she was picking flowers in a field in Sicily, the ground suddenly split open.

- **Out of the ground** sprang Hades, the god of the underworld, and of death. He grabbed the beautiful Kore and hauled her into his chariot, then plunged back down beneath the Earth.

- **Hades took Kore** to the underworld where he married her and changed her name to Persephone, queen of the Underworld.

- **Demeter did not know** what had happened to her daughter and was terribly upset. She wandered the Earth looking for Kore and ignored her divine duties of helping the crops to grow.

- **All mankind suffered** as plants did not grow and cold winter gripped the land. Finally, Zeus ordered Hades to give up Kore, but Kore had eaten four pomegranate seeds, which meant she would have to return to Hades for four months of each year. These four months became winter.

- **It was believed** that Kore returned to Earth and to Demeter by climbing out of the ground at Eleusis, and the Mysteries celebrated this.

- **The festival began** with a great procession from Athens to the sea, where several pigs were sacrificed. The procession then continued to Eleusis.

▶ *Hades, king of the underworld, takes Persephone down to his kingdom to be his wife, bringing winter to Earth.*

● **On arrival at Eleusis,** the procession divided. Most people waited outside the temple grounds, but those who had been chosen by the priestess of Demeter could enter.

● **Inside the temple,** a play was staged and sacrifices were made. There was then a great feast.

The cults

- **In addition** to the official Olympian gods and the public ceremonies carried out at temples, the Greeks also had a number of cults.

- **A cult** was a club or society that was dedicated to the worship of one particular god. Membership of these societies was often kept secret. Many had specific rituals and beliefs that were unknown outside the cult.

- **The wine god**, Dionysus, was the focus of a very popular cult. Dionysus was officially worshipped only once a year, at the Dionysian festival in the spring, but his cult continued all year round.

- **Women took part** in the cultic ceremony of Dionysus. They would meet in a wood, where they drank large quantities of wine, and danced. After this, they ate a meal of raw meat.

▶ *Isis was a goddess in Egyptian mythology, where she was worshipped as a wife and mother figure. She became the centre of a popular cult in later Greek times.*

196

- **The women's cultic ceremony** of Dionysus was based on a legend of
semi-divine women, called Maenads, who were said to follow the god in
a wild dance. It was believed that they would tear to pieces anyone who
did not worship the god.

- **Men who took part** in the Dionysus cult attended ceremonies held in
private houses. These usually involved drinking huge quantities of wine.

- **During the Hellenistic Period**, the Persian god Mithras became the
focus for a new cult. Mithras was a sun god who helped crops grow, and
was linked to fertility.

- **The cult ceremonies** of Mithras took place in caves or underground
rooms, in which a statue of Mithras killing a bull was placed. Rituals
included sacred meals of roasted meat.

- **The Egyptian goddess**, Isis, was the centre for a cult in Greece that
appears to have catered mostly for women and travellers.

The oracle of Delphi

- **At Delphi**, on a mountainside overlooking the Gulf of Corinth, stood a temple to Apollo that was one of the most famous and respected in the whole Greek world.

- **The fame of Delphi** was due to the fact that the chief priestess was believed to be able to talk directly to Apollo, to ask him questions on behalf of the humans who visited the temple.

- **A place** where humans could talk to the gods was known as an oracle. The oracle at Delphi was considered to be the greatest in the world.

◄ *A small shrine at Delphi, where the god Apollo was thought to answer questions posed by humans.*

- **According to legend**, Apollo killed a terrible serpent named Python at Delphi. To celebrate this feat, he set up an altar to himself and persuaded a group of sailors from Crete to settle there as his priests.

- **People who wished** to consult the god at Delphi had to climb the mountain and bathe in the waters of a sacred spring. They were then allowed into the sacred precincts of the temple.

- **After waiting for the chief priestess**, the Pythia, to announce she was ready, the men were led into the temple and through to a small, dark room near the back. Here, they told the Pythia the question that they wanted to ask Apollo.

- **The Pythia** then stood on a three-legged stool that spanned a crack in the rocks, from which came volcanic gasses. The Pythia fell into a trance, during which she was believed to become possessed by Apollo.

- **The Pythia's answer** came in one of several forms. Sometimes she answered the question in verse, sometimes in ordinary speech and sometimes by incoherent rantings, which were translated by a priest.

- **The answers given** by the oracle at Delphi are often said to have been either obscure or to have two meanings. King Croesus was told that if he invaded Persia he would destroy a mighty kingdom. He did, but the kingdom that was destroyed was his own, and not Persia.

- **Some answers were very clear.** In 480 BC, the oracle told a representative from Athens, "pray to the winds". The Athenians did, and a storm destroyed much of the Persian invasion fleet.

The Panathenaea

- **One of the most impressive ceremonies** held in ancient Greece was the Panathenaea. It was held in Athens once a year. A larger celebration called the Great Panathenaea was held every four years.

- **The Panathenaea** was held in honour of the goddess Athene, who was the patron goddess of Athens. Athene was the goddess of wisdom, but she was also a warrior who would protect Athens.

- **It is thought the Panathenaea** was first held in Mycenaean times, perhaps around 1600 BC. It continued to be held for nearly 2000 years, until it was banned when Christianity took over.

- **The main purpose** of the Panathenaea was to present the goddess with a new cloak, which was draped around her statue on the Acropolis. The cloak was made by the finest weaver in the city.

- **The ceremony began** when the weaver handed the cloak to the chief priestess of Athene. The priestess then took her place at the head of a long procession.

- **The word 'Panathenaea'** means 'all-Athens'. The procession included all the priests of Athens, together with magistrates and government officials. There were also young women carrying baskets, old men carrying olive branches and young aristocrats on fine horses.

- **The procession** wound through the streets of Athens, then climbed the Acropolis to halt outside the temple of Athene. The chief priestess then entered the temple and draped the cloak over the statue, where it remained for four years.

- **After this central ceremony**, others took place. There were musical and and dancing contests. Ship races were held in the harbour at Piraeus.

- **The Panathenian procession** was recorded in a series of carvings that were put up just under the roof of the temple of Athene (the Parthenon).

- **The first statue** of Athene was made of wood, but it was destroyed during the Persian Wars. A new statue of ivory and gold was built that stood over 6 m tall.

▼ *The Erechtheion on the Acropolis, Athens, was built to honour the legendary founders of the city. The procession of the Panathenaea made its way up the slopes of the Acropolis and passed in front of this building.*

The Olympic Games

- **The most important** shrine to Zeus was at Olympia in the western Peloponnese, between the Kronos hill and the river Kladeos.

- **Once every four years**, men from all Greek *poleis* gathered at Olympia to watch or take part in athletic competitions, which were held in honour of Zeus. Physical prowess was believed to be a gift from the gods.

- **Some ancient Greeks** believed the Olympic Games were founded in about 1480 BC by Zeus, while others thought they were started by Heracles in 1222 BC.

- **The first recorded games** were held in 776 BC. There was only one event, a foot race, which was won by a man named Coroebus of Elis.

- **For many years** the foot race was the only event, but gradually other contests were added. One of the most taxing events was the pentathlon. Contestants taking part competed in five different sports – running, wrestling, the long jump, throwing the discus and throwing the javelin.

- **Some popular events** were derived from warfare. Discus-throwing developed from throwing shaped stones in battle. Horse and chariot races were staged on a special track called a hippodrome.

- **The governments** of *poleis* gave rewards to citizens who won at Olympia. They might be freed from paying taxes for life, given money, or allowed to sit in the front row for all theatre shows and religious festivals.

> ...FASCINATING FACT...
> The finest athletes from across the Greek world competed at the Olympic Games, and the prestige of winning was immense, but the only prize given was a wreath of olive leaves for the winner of each event.

▼ *The entrance to the stadium at Olympia. Athletes walked down this passageway to reach the competition grounds.*

● **Women were not permitted** to compete in the Olympic Games. Instead, they held their own version, the games of Hera.

● **The Olympic Games** were banned in AD 391 by the Roman emperor, Theodosius I, who was a Christian.

Sacred games

- **Most of the events** of the Olympic Games were held in a special stadium that was built beside the hill of Kronos. At first, spectators sat on the hillside but later, benches were erected.

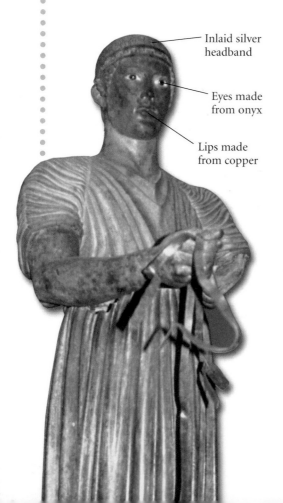

Inlaid silver headband

Eyes made from onyx

Lips made from copper

- **The judges** sat in a special stand half-way along the southern side of the stadium. They had to judge who had won each race, and penalize anyone who broke the rules.

- **Winners were allowed** to erect a statue or monument to themselves as a mark of gratitude to Apollo for their success.

- **Some cities** chose to donate treasures or trophies for display at Olympia. The city of Athens donated the helmet of Miltiadies, the general who won the Battle of Marathon.

◀ *The well-preserved charioteer found at Delphi is one of the finest examples of ancient bronze statues. Statues were erected to honour the most successful athletes.*

- **The objects donated** to Olympia were stored in small buildings known as treasuries, which lined the north side of the sacred precinct. Some *poleis* had their own treasury, others shared a building with other states.

- **The Olympic Games** were not the only games held in ancient Greece. Other games were held at Delphi and Athens.

- **The ancient Greeks believed** that the site of Delphi was sacred to the god Apollo, and the Pythian Games were held there every four years in his honour. The games were held in a stadium carved out of the mountainside, just above the temple of Apollo. The events were very similar to those of the Olympic Games, and included running and chariot races.

- **As at Olympia**, winners were allowed to put up a statue of themselves if they wished. In AD 58, the Roman emperor Nero visited Greece and was so impressed by the statues at Delphi that he had 500 of them shipped to Rome to decorate his palace.

- **Corinth organized the Isthmian Games**. Isthmus was believed to be the sanctuary of the god Poseidon, and games were held there every two years to honour him and a local sea god called Melicerta.

- **The Isthmian Games** are said to have been founded in 1326 BC, although the earliest recorded games were held some 700 years later. After Corinth was destroyed in 146 BC by the Romans, the games were organized by the city of Sicyon.

The kingdom of the dead

- **Funerals in ancient Greece** could be very grand. The body was carefully washed, and dressed in a white robe. It was then laid out on a bed in a room of the house where the person had lived.

- **After one day**, during which friends and relatives could visit to pay their respects, the body was carried to the burial grounds. A rich person's body would be transported on a carriage.

- **The funeral procession** included musicians, and professional mourners who were paid to wail and weep as loudly as possible. The family and friends of the dead person followed behind.

- **Bodies were buried or cremated** (**burned**). Most families had a tomb in which the body or ashes of their dead relatives would be buried. The living relative would visit the tomb regularly to pay respects and make offerings to the dead.

- **The Greeks believed** that the souls of the dead went to the underworld, which was ruled by the god Hades.

- **To reach Hades**, the dead soul had to be ferried across the River Styx by Charon, the ferryman. Charon charged for the service, so most people were buried with a bronze coin.

- **Once past the River Styx**, a dead person had to get past the three-headed dog, Cerberus, which stopped the living entering the underworld, or the dead leaving.

- **On arrival into the underworld**, the soul was met by Hades, brother to Zeus and king of the dead. Along with Hades, were the souls of King Minos of Crete, and King Rhadamanthys of the Cyclades, both of whom had been famous for justice when alive.

- **Hades, Minos and Rhadmanthys** questioned the souls that came before them. Those who had offended the gods were imprisoned behind bronze gates, in Tartarus, where they were tortured for eternity. Most souls went to the underworld, which was a grey, dull place.

- **The souls** of those who had pleased the gods were sent to the Elysian Fields. This was a sunny, beautiful country swept by warm, gentle breezes, where good food and wine was plentiful.

◀ *The supernatural dog, Cerberus, had three heads. The Greeks thought that this dog guarded the entrance to the lands of the dead.*

207

Index

Index

Index

Index

Index

Index

Index